Seasons of Change

GOD'S FAITHFULNESS
IN THE LIFE OF RUTH

MICHELLE ELAINE BURTON

FIRST EDITION

ISBN 978-1-7360079-0-7 (Paperback)
ISBN 978-1-7360079-1-4 (eBook)

*For the ladies of Faith Baptist Church in Layton, Utah.
I pray that these words will encourage your hearts in
the same way that your words encouraged my heart
in the three and a half years I had the privilege of
being with you.*

Today for God's glory
And not for my own,
I'm telling a story
With talents He has loaned.

CONTENTS

INTRODUCTION

I hate change. But life seems to be full of change, whether I invite it or not. The idea for this book was born in the midst of an exciting change. I had just married my husband, Steven, and we were driving across the country from sunny Tennessee to snowy Utah in the middle of January. I suppose the idea must have been stirring in my head for quite some time, but it was during that quiet time in the U-Haul that I vocalized the thing that God was leading me to do: write a study on the book of Ruth.

The story slowly unfolded onto pages in the coming months and years. Three and a half years later, we were surprised to find ourselves moving back to Tennessee following God's leading for my husband to serve at a church as youth pastor. On the return journey, we had a baby in tow, as well as a finished study on the book of Ruth. As we made the trip to the hot and humid South in the middle of the summer, I knew that the time was drawing near for the words God had led me to write to be published.

Through all the changes in my life, I know this one thing: God has remained the same. Ruth also faced dramatic changes in her life, but the God she came to know through them all was an unchanging constant in the midst of her ever-changing world. My prayer as you read this book is that you will find comfort and stability in that same unchanging God. No matter what circumstances you are facing, He is always the same, yesterday, today, and forever. Even if you don't understand what He is doing in your life right now, He is always at work behind the scenes, and His plan for your life is very good.

Chapter One

WHEN GOD CHANGES YOUR PLANS

I'll follow God's plan
And turn away from mine;
Though I don't understand,
I know He'll show me in time.

The book of Ruth is often thought of as one of the most captivating love stories in the Bible, and it truly is. However, there are more love stories in this book than just the story of Ruth and Boaz, even though that is inevitably the story we think of when the book of Ruth comes to mind. It's easy to forget that the book opens with neither Ruth nor Boaz mentioned as characters. At the beginning of the book of Ruth, we meet a little family from Bethlehem.

Ruth 1:1-3
Now it came to pass in the days when the judges

ruled, that there was a famine in the land. And a certain man of Bethlehem-judah went to sojourn in the country of Moab, he and his wife, and his two sons. And the name of the man was Elimelech, and the name of his wife Naomi, and the name of his two sons Mahlon and Chilion, Ephrathites of Bethlehem-judah. And they came into the country of Moab, and continued there. And Elimelech Naomi's husband died; and she was left, and her two sons.

Here we meet a man, Elimelech, who is simply trying to do what he felt was best for his family. However, God never intended for them to leave Bethlehem. Their happy little family was soon divided by an untimely death. The characters of our story are now a grieving widow and two fatherless sons. It is this tragic context in which we meet Ruth.

Ruth 1:4-5
And they took them wives of the women of Moab; the name of the one was Orpah and the name of the other Ruth: and they dwelled there about ten years. And Mahlon and Chilion died also both of them; and the woman was left of her two sons and her husband.

You have probably all heard of the story of Ruth and Boaz. But what about the story of Ruth and Mahlon? I can hear you now: "How is that a love story? We hardly know anything about Ruth and Mahlon other than that they got married, and then he died. That's not much of a love story." And you're right. The Bible doesn't tell us much about this first marriage of Ruth, but I'm sure your imagination could help you out a little bit without adding anything to the truth. After all, how many times over the years has your imagination been the author of a beautiful love story?

Imagine with me: There's a young girl named Ruth. Just like any girl in her time, she longs to find love and be married. She wants to have a family. She believes this will be truly fulfilling to her. But in her heart is the doubt that has plagued many women: will I ever get married? Then one day, Mahlon, the handsome Israelite, comes into the picture. He sweeps her off her feet, and she believes they will live happily ever after. Sounds dreamy, doesn't it? Ten years pass. Ruth grows to love this man, and even has a desire to follow the God of his people. They hadn't had any children, but there was plenty of time for that. Right? Ruth probably had her life planned out. Sadly, tragedy was about to enter her life in a way she had never imagined. Suddenly, her beloved husband was gone.

Plans change. We don't like it when plans change. We like it when we have everything figured out, and we know exactly what's going to happen next. But hasn't there been a time in all of our lives when God changed our plans? I know there has been such a time in my life.

My freshman year of college was especially hard for me. I was away from home for the very first time. I tried to be strong on the outside, but on the inside I was falling apart. God was in the process of changing my plans. When you move away, relationships change. I grew apart from many friends on whom I had come to depend. I felt like God was taking everything from me that I had ever loved. I had lost everything in life that I looked to for fulfillment. I felt completely hopeless. I'm sure Ruth felt much the same way.

When God changes our plans, we have two choices. The first choice is to turn away from God and try to find satisfaction somewhere else. The second choice is to turn to God and trust that He has a plan far greater than anything we ever could have imagined for ourselves. This second option is always the best option, and it is the choice that Ruth made. The next passage in the book of Ruth is a very familiar one. Within it, we see a contrast: two women faced with the same choice. Only one woman made the right choice, the choice to turn to God.

Ruth 1:6-17
Then she arose with her daughters in law, that she might return from the country of Moab: for she had heard in the country of Moab how that the LORD had visited his people in giving them bread. Wherefore she went forth out of the place where

*she was, and her two daughters in law with her;
and they went on the way to return unto the land
of Judah. And Naomi said unto her two daughters
in law, Go, return each to her mother's house: the
LORD deal kindly with you, as ye have dealt with
the dead, and with me. The LORD grant you that
ye may find rest, each of you in the house of her
husband. Then she kissed them; and they lifted
up their voice, and wept. And they said unto her,
Surely we will return with thee unto thy people.
And Naomi said, Turn again, my daughters: why
will ye go with me? are there yet any more sons in
my womb, that they may be your husbands? Turn
again, my daughters, go your way; for I am too old
to have an husband. If I should say, I have hope,
if I should have an husband also to night, and
should also bear sons; Would ye tarry for them
till they were grown? would ye stay for them from
having husbands? nay, my daughters; for it grie-
veth me much for your sakes that the hand of the
LORD is gone out against me. And they lifted up
their voice, and wept again: and Orpah kissed her
mother in law; but Ruth clave unto her. And she
said, Behold, thy sister in law is gone back unto
her people, and unto her gods: return thou after
thy sister in law. And Ruth said, Intreat me not
to leave thee, or to return from following after
thee: for whither thou goest, I will go; and where*

thou lodgest, 1 will lodge: thy people shall be my people, and thy God my God: Where thou diest, will 1 die, and there will 1 be buried: the LORD do so to me, and more also, if ought but death part thee and me.

Both of these young women were given the same choice. Orpah chose to try to find satisfaction on her own, without God. Ruth made the wise choice in choosing to follow Naomi, and, in turn, follow God. Every person on earth is faced with this same choice. 1 was faced with this choice during my difficult time of transitioning into college.

1 finished my freshman year and started my sophomore year, still without the hope 1 so desperately needed. Most people who were close to me realized there was something wrong, but almost nobody could have guessed what the real problem was. It all came down to the choice Ruth and Orpah had to make. 1 had never really chosen to follow God, and the moment of decision had come for me.

1 had so many people fooled. Growing up, everyone thought 1 was the "good Christian girl." 1 always went to church, 1 had read through the Bible both in English and Spanish, and 1 even wanted to be a missionary! 1 was preparing to be a Bible translator and bring God's Word to people who had never before been able to read it in their native language. How could 1 possibly not be a Christian? God doesn't save

us because we pray, because we're good, because we go to church, or even because we want to do something great for Him. God saves us only when we put our faith in the finished work of Jesus on the cross to save us. In that first semester of my sophomore year of college, I chose to do just that. I stopped trusting a prayer that I prayed as a child (that I don't even remember praying), the moral life I was living (at least it was moral outwardly), or the determination in my heart to become a Bible translator, and I chose to put my trust in Jesus and Jesus alone.

I can assure you, putting your faith in Jesus is the best decision you will ever make. It will completely change your life for the better. However, I can't assure you that the change will always be easy. At first, the changes God wants to make in your life may be difficult. You may want to resist the changes. But if we truly want to live a fulfilled life in Christ, it is so vital that we embrace the changes He wants to make in us.

Some of the changes God wants to make in your life may be more general, things He wants for everybody. Maybe God wants you to start doing something like going to church regularly, having a regular time of Bible reading and prayer, or being a witness for Him. These are all things that He wants every Christian to be actively doing! Or maybe God wants you to stop being involved in some things. Maybe there is a sin that is so ingrained in your heart, but through the power of the cross, God wants you to give that up. Maybe it's greed, discontentment, gossip, or habitual lying. Whatever it is, God will without a doubt prompt you to get rid of the sin that has you so captivated. These are all very general changes that God requires of everyone. However, there may be more specific changes God has in store for you.

God's will. We hear about it all the time. Sometimes it seems like it's this nebulous concept, not something really concrete. But God really does have a plan for each individual life! After you entrust your life to Him, He absolutely wants you to know what His perfect plan is for your life. He won't show you all at once, but I can assure you, if you seek Him, He will start to show you the next steps He has for you. However, you must be prepared that God's plan for your life may not be exactly what you had imagined it would be. That may sound scary, but it's actually not scary at all! Why are we so insistent on planning our own lives with our finite knowledge when the omniscient, Creator God wants to guide our lives into the most wonderful plan that He can possibly think of for us?

> *1 Corinthians 2:19*
> *But as it is written, Eye hath not seen, nor ear heard, neither have entered into the heart of man, the things which God hath prepared for them that love him.*

What a beautiful way to describe God's plan for the lives of his children! Why is it so difficult for us to entrust our lives to a God who loves us so much? Perhaps it's because we think our plan for our own life is already pretty good. I thought my plan to be a missionary was pretty good, but after I accepted Christ as my Savior, I had to really consider if that was what God wanted for my life. I know it was no coincidence that the day after I got saved my Sunday school teacher, Miss Nicole Torberson, taught a lesson about "God's will."

The beginning of the lesson was about the general will of God, the things I mentioned that we know God wants us to do because He commands it in His Word. The end of the lesson was what I was really interested in hearing about: God's specific will for my life. What Miss Torberson told us about how to find God's specific will and the verse that supported her conclusion became the driving force behind my search for God's purpose for my life. This is what she told us: "If you are already following the things God has commanded us to do in His Word, then God's will for your life is for you to do whatever you want."

What? I thought this was supposed to be about doing what God wants! Do whatever I want? That doesn't make any sense! Oh, but it does make sense. Let's see what God's Word has to say about it:

Psalm 37:4
Delight thyself also in the LORD: and he shall give
thee the desires of thine heart.

When we are delighting in God by living a life of obedience to Him, He will place within our hearts the desires He wants us to have. When we follow those desires that are given to us by God, we can know for sure that we are following God's will. I left Sunday school that day with a commitment to delight in the Lord daily and with the confidence that if God wanted to use my life in a way other than serving on a foreign mission field, He would change the desires of my heart. Little did I know just how greatly He would change my plans.

God revealed His will for my life slowly at first, and then He turned my life upside down all at once. It started with God teaching me that His heart was not just for people on a foreign mission field; His heart was for people everywhere. He changed my heart and made me realize that it didn't really matter where I ended up in life; serving Him is never limited to a location. However, because I still didn't know exactly what God wanted for my life, I continued doing what I was already doing: preparing to be a Bible translator. It was one day while I was sitting in Greek class working on my translations that God turned my life upside down and changed my plans in a way that I never could have imagined.

I was quietly doing my translations when I heard the still, small voice of the Holy Spirit more loudly than I ever had before or than I ever have since. He clearly said, *"This is not what I made you to do."* What? Then why was I there? I wasn't doubting my future as a Bible translator because Greek was suddenly difficult for me; I actually made very good grades. It wasn't that I suddenly disliked languages. My interest in language learning and translation was as strong as it ever had been. It was just that the moment had finally come for God to stop me in my tracks and completely change my plans.

Greek was my last class of the day, so as soon as class was dismissed, I went straight to my room and did the only thing I knew how to do in that moment: I opened my Bible and prayed with an open heart that God would show me what it was He wanted me to do, and He did exactly that. By the end of that afternoon, God had made it clear to me through His Word and through the desires He had been placing in my heart over the previous year that the thing He had made me to do was simply to be a wife and mother.

Talk about a change of plans! I can't say that I was too happy about it at first, but I knew that was how God was leading. It didn't make much sense to me, and I struggled with surrender at first. However, I never doubted that it was God's leading.

Following God's will isn't just a one time decision;

it's an every day decision. He may reveal His will for one season of your life and then completely change your plans. He doesn't map out His will for your life all at once; His will most often comes in pieces. But if we are faithful to follow His will, at the end of our lives all the pieces will make a picture more beautiful than we could have ever imagined.

Maybe you are in a season right now where God is changing your plans. Please keep your heart open to the things God is doing in your life. He knows far more than we do, and His plan is always for our good. Ultimately, our lives are not about "us." Our lives are about bringing glory to God.

1 Corinthians 10:31
Whether therefore ye eat, or drink, or whatsoever
ye do, do all to the glory of God.

QUESTIONS FOR DISCUSSION

1. Has there been a time in your life when you have made the decision that Ruth made to follow God? What are you trusting for your salvation? Are you trusting a prayer or your good works? Or are you trusting Jesus?

2. Describe a time in your life when God has changed your plans.

3. What are some practical ways you can start following God's general will for your life today?

4. Has God ever revealed to you a piece of His specific will for your life? If so, what was the thing He revealed to you?

5. Is there a desire that you know God has placed in your heart? What action steps can you take to start living out that God-given desire?

Chapter 2

WHAT'S IN A NAME?

To have a good name
Is worth far more
Than all personal gain,
For that name shall endure.

The next few verses set the scene within which the rest of our story will take place. Much to Ruth's delight, Naomi allowed Ruth to accompany her back to her homeland of Bethlehem. However, it wasn't with the joy of an appreciative and loving mother-in-law that Naomi accepted Ruth's insistence; Naomi's acceptance was simply a silent apathy and a lack of spirit left within her to make an argument.

Ruth 1:18
When she saw that she was stedfastly minded to go with her, then she left speaking unto her.

Naomi realized there was nothing she could say or do to prevent Ruth from following her, so she simply let come what may.

The years in Moab had changed Naomi. She had allowed the hardships she faced there to define who she was as a person. It didn't take long for her old friends in Bethlehem to recognize that this was not the Naomi they once knew.

Ruth 1:19
So they two went until they came to Bethlehem. And it came to pass, when they were come to Bethlehem, that all the city was moved about them, and they said, is this Naomi?

I can imagine Naomi's countenance had changed in such a way that she was barely recognizable. Her response reveals the change in her heart as well. We see her true brokenness in her response to her friends.

Ruth 1:20-21
And she said unto them, Call me not Naomi, call me Mara: for the Almighty hath dealt very bitterly with me. I went out full, and the LORD hath brought me home empty: why then call ye me Naomi, seeing the LORD hath testified against me, and the Almighty hath afflicted me?

When parents today choose names for their children, there could be a number of reasons behind the names. Perhaps you were named for a relative or a family friend; that's the case with my name. It's possible that your parents picked your name just because they liked the way it sounded. However, in Bible times, Hebrew parents were a little more intentional about picking names for their children. The names they picked usually had a deep meaning, often surrounding the events of the child's birth. It was very important for these Hebrew children to live up to their names. My name, Michelle, is from the Hebrew and means "who is like God." That's definitely a name I want to live up to! Naomi's name means "pleasantness." I believe that in her early years, this name was very defining of her lifestyle; she was most likely a very pleasant person to be around. However, life in Moab had changed her so much she felt it would be most appropriate to change her name.

Mara. It means bitter. What a sad commentary on Naomi's life that she felt she was no longer defined by pleasantness, but was defined by bitterness. She felt like God had forsaken her, and she no longer believed He had a good plan for her life. This is the state in which we find her as she settles into her life in Bethlehem with Ruth.

Ruth 1:22
So Naomi returned, and Ruth the Moabitess, her daughter in law, with her, which returned out of the country of Moab: and they came to Bethlehem

in the beginning of barley harvest.

And there they were, all alone together in Bethlehem. A widowed stranger from a heathen land, and a woman whose life was so defined by bitterness that she herself was a stranger to her friends. This doesn't seem like the perfect setup for a beautiful story, but we can't forget that God *always* has a beautiful plan for our lives. Even when we can't see it.

Although we don't always choose the names of our children for a special reason anymore, there are definitely some names that we as women should try to live up to. How about the name of "Christian"? God's followers weren't always called Christians; in fact, they weren't the first to call themselves Christians!

Acts 11:26
...And the disciples were called Christians first in Antioch.

The first people to give the name "Christian" to the followers of Christ were not followers of Christ themselves! The word they invented simply means "one who is of Christ." The Christians so closely identified with Christ and were so much like Him that there was a clear difference in their lives in the eyes of the unbelievers. They were obviously living up to the name of "Christian" because it was their lifestyle that earned them that name to begin with.

Are you living up to the name of "Christian"? What

would your family say? How about your coworkers or the people you go to school with? The name of "Christian" is the most important name we have to live up to. As women, there are many other names that we may be called to live up to over the course of our lives. Perhaps the first name is "daughter." This name isn't something we choose, but rather a name that we take on the moment we are born. I don't know your parents; I don't know what your relationship with them is like. But I do know that God has given us certain commandments to follow as daughters.

> *Ephesians 6:1*
> *Children, obey your parents in the Lord: for this is right.*

If you are a teenager still living at home, this verse is for you. You may not think of yourself as a child anymore, but there are still so many things that you don't know (whether you realize it or not). God has put your parents in your life to help you navigate these years of learning and decision making. If your parents tell you to do something (unless it clearly goes against what God says in the Bible), it is because they have your best interest at heart. Obedience is still for you! If you choose obedience, you will save yourself from many regrets later in life when you look back on your teenage years.

What about those of us who are grown and no

longer living with our parents? How can we be good daughters? The Bible tells us in the very next verse.

Ephesians 6:2
Honor thy father and mother; (which is the first commandment with promise;)

If you are an adult and are no longer living at home with your parents, God does not call you to continue to obey your parents. However, He does call you to *honor* them. This simply means we are to show *respect* to our parents. Just because we no longer have to obey our parents doesn't mean they don't often know more than we do. One of the best ways to honor your parents is by continuing to seek their counsel, even though you don't have to. God will bless you for showing respect to your parents! In fact, He says that this commandment comes with a promise!

Ephesians 6:3
That it may be well with thee, and thou mayest live long on the earth.

The promise that comes with this commandment is a long life! Who wouldn't want a long life? Living up to the name of a good daughter is so important, even though that is a name we did not choose. However, after becoming a daughter, many of the names we have in life are things we *did* choose. The first name that comes to mind is "wife." You may have taken on that name so long ago that you don't remember choosing to become a wife. In fact, you may wish you hadn't made that choice. But you did. And God calls us to live up to that name in a way that is pleasing to Him.

Ephesians 5:22
Wives, submit yourselves unto your own husbands, as unto the Lord.

The greatest duty of a wife as found in the Bible can be summed up in one word: *submission.* I can tell you that this definitely isn't a popular concept anymore, but God never said that following His Word would be popular. In a world full of radical feminism that tells us submission is a sign of weakness, God still calls us to submit. But submission doesn't have to be a bad thing! I sincerely hope you have a wonderful, godly husband like I do. If you do, submission is an absolutely wonderful thing! I count it a privilege to be able to follow my husband as He follows the Lord's leading for our lives. I am thankful for the guidance and protection God has provided for me in the form of my husband's leadership. God designed women to have a need to be cared for, loved, and led. When we submit to our husbands, we find that such is the means through which those needs are met.

Perhaps you don't have a godly husband. God still calls you to submit to him.

1 Peter 3:1
Likewise, ye wives, be in subjection to your own husbands; that, if any obey not the word, they also may without the word be won by the conversation of the wives;

God tells us that our godly lifestyle and submission to our husbands can actually be the catalyst that causes an unsaved husband to turn to Christ! The Bible doesn't say how long this will take; perhaps it will take years. Don't give up hope. Keep obeying God's command to submit, and He will bless you for it.

Perhaps you have chosen to take the name of "mother." Or maybe you didn't choose; maybe motherhood came as a surprise to you. Whatever the case may be, if you are a mother, God wants you to live up to that name in a way that is pleasing to Him.

Ephesians 6:4
And, ye fathers, provoke not your children to wrath: but bring them up in the nurture and admonition of the Lord.

This verse is for fathers *and* mothers! If God has entrusted you with children, He is calling you to raise them up in a way that is pleasing to Him! The only way to do this is by knowing what He says about raising children in His Word. I won't go into this subject in great detail; an entire book could be written on what God's Word says about raising children! In fact, many books have been written on the subject. I would encourage you, first of all, to search the Scriptures to see what God has to say about raising children *in the nurture and admonition of the Lord.* I would also encourage you to seek out Scripture based books on the subject. Be diligent to study, and God will reveal to you how to parent in a way that is pleasing to Him.

Another name you may have chosen is "employee." At some point in your life, you will probably be in a position in which you are working for someone. If we look in Ephesians, God has a few things to say about how we should live up to the name of "employee" as well.

Ephesians 6:5-8
Servants, be obedient to them that are your masters according to the flesh, with fear and trembling, in singleness of your heart, as unto Christ; not with eyeservice, as menpleasers; but as the servants of Christ, doing the will of God from the heart; with good will doing service, as to the Lord, and not to men: knowing that whatsoever good thing any man doth, the same shall he receive of the Lord, whether he be bond or free.

The words used in these verses are "servant" and "master," but they would really be the equivalent of today's "employee" and "employer." God actually tells us that we are to obey our employers! Again, the exception here is if your employer is asking you to do something that directly contradicts God's commands in the Bible, like lying or stealing. Otherwise, we are to do what our employers ask us to do, and we are to do it with a good attitude. This may be difficult, especially if you have an employer who is unpleasant to work with. However, God provides us with a motivation that will help us follow this command regardless of the difficulties we encounter. We can cheerfully obey our employers because we know we are not really serving them; we are serving the Lord. Everything we do in life is for the purpose of glorifying God.

Colossians 3:17
And whatsoever ye do in word or deed, do all in the name of the Lord Jesus, giving thanks to God and the Father by him.

1 Corinthians 10:31
Whether therefore ye eat, or drink, or whatsoever ye do, do all to the glory of God.

When we stop doing our work with the purpose of pleasing our employers and start doing it with the intention of glorifying God, there will be a noticeable change in our work ethic.

Perhaps you are the "boss." God has something to say about how to live up to that name as well.

Ephesians 6:9
And, ye masters, do the same things unto them,
forbearing threatening: knowing that your Master
also is in heaven; neither is there respect of per-
sons with him.

The key here is kindness. Unfortunately, many bosses believe that a harsh spirit that strikes fear into the hearts of employees is the most effective way to manage, but the Bible tells us that the exact opposite is true. First of all, you are also to be doing your work as service to the Lord, not to impress men. Second, this passage specifically tells employers not to use threats as a way to motivate their workers. They are also reminded that they have a Master as well: their Master is God. Treating others the way God has treated you will always go a long way.

Ephesians 4:32
And be ye kind one to another, tenderhearted, for-
giving one another, even as God for Christ's sake
hath forgiven you.

God has treated us with the ultimate kindness; we should always treat others with that same kindness. My dad has been in management in the food industry for many years. In recent years, I have had the opportunity to meet quite a few of his employees from years gone by. Of the many words they have used to describe him, one stands out as a common theme of all their descriptions: kind. I want to always have that same kindness in my own life.

I know I have barely scratched the surface of the many names you may have in this life, but I hope I have given you something to ponder. Living up to the names you have been given in life in a way that brings glory to God is a priceless thing.

Proverbs 22:1
A good name is rather to be chosen than great riches, and loving favour rather than silver and gold.

QUESTIONS FOR DISCUSSION

1. Do you know why your parents chose your name?

2. Do you know the meaning of your name? If not, take a minute to look it up.

3. What are some practical ways you could be a better Christian? A better daughter? A better wife? A better mother? A better worker? A better leader?

4. What are some names that describe you that were not mentioned in this chapter? What are some practical ways you could live up to those names?

Chapter 3

COINCIDENCE? I THINK NOT!

It seemed like coincidence,
But I now understand:
Each and every event is
Part of God's perfect plan.

Our stage has been set. Ruth and Naomi have made their home in Bethlehem. So now what would Ruth do? Would she just have to sit around at home with Naomi and wait for God to give her some sort of divine revelation as to what His next step for her was? Of course not! While we are waiting for God to show us His will, there will always be something He has for us to do. Ruth made the wise choice to pursue what she knew God had for her next.

Ruth 2:1-3
And Naomi had a kinsman of her husband's, a

mighty man of wealth, of the family of Elimelech;
and his name was Boaz. And Ruth the Moabitess
said unto Naomi, Let me now go to the field, and
glean ears of corn after him in whose sight I shall
find grace. And she said unto her, Go, my daugh-
ter. And she went, and came, and gleaned in the
field after the reapers: and her hap was to light on
a part of the field belonging unto Boaz, who was
of the kindred of Elimelech.

I love these verses! First of all, we see a little fore-shadowing of the love story that's about to unfold. But Ruth doesn't know anything about that yet, so we'll have to wait to see it unfold as she does. Ruth makes the decision to fulfill her responsibilities to her mother-in-law. She had made a commitment to be with her mother-in-law and help her, and she was going to be faithful to that commitment. No matter what that meant.

Gleaning. It wasn't easy work; it wasn't glamorous work. But it was the work God had provided for Ruth to do. It was the work of poor people, the work of widows and strangers. But God made specific provision for this work in the law.

Leviticus 23:22
And when ye reap the harvest of your land, thou
shalt not make clean riddance of the corners of
thy field when thou reapest, neither shalt thou

gather any gleaning of thy harvest: thou shalt leave them unto the poor, and to the stranger: I am the Lord your God.

Deuteronomy 24:19
When thou cuttest down thine harvest in thy field, and hast forgot a sheaf in the field, thou shalt not go again to fetch it: it shall be for the stranger, for the fatherless, and for the widow: that the Lord thy God may bless thee in all the work of thine hands.

Even though it wasn't easy, Ruth decided to take advantage of a provision God had already made. He had commanded that the scraps of each harvest should be left alone so that the foreigners in the land, such as Ruth, would be able to find food. It was the beginning of barley harvest. So what did Ruth do? She found a barley field. She followed the reapers. She gathered the leftovers. The scraps. The rejects. That doesn't sound like a whole lot of fun to me.

But what's this I see? A coincidence? *"Her hap was to light on a part of the field belonging unto Boaz, who was of the kindred of Elimelech."* Oh, now it just so happens, she picks the part of the barley field that belongs to a relative of her late husband. How about that. What a crazy coincidence!

You and I would both be naïve to think that this was simply a coincidence. It also wasn't of Ruth's own scheming. She didn't know who her late husband's kinsmen were! She had never even been to Bethlehem before! No, this was a divine work of God, providing for Ruth when she didn't even realize it.

As I look back on my life, there seem to have been a lot of crazy coincidences that brought me to the place God has me in today. However, I know that nothing in life is a coincidence. I know that each event in my life was divinely orchestrated by God so that He could put me right where he wanted me serving alongside my husband in his ministry. Who knew it would start with an eight year old girl who wanted nothing more than to go to the mission field?

It seems crazy to think that my burning desire to be a missionary in the Philippines would be exactly the thing that put me on the path to marriage and ministry in America. Apart from God, it seems like a series of crazy coincidences. But I'm glad my life doesn't operate apart from God; it operates exactly according to His plan.

Because of my desire to be a missionary in the Philippines, a couple in my church offered to take me on a missions trip with them so I could see the country in which I planned to spend the rest of my life. I was only sixteen at the time, but my parents were completely supportive. We were all sure that it was what God wanted. However, the plans of the couple I intended to travel with were changed. They still wanted me to have the opportunity to go to the

Philippines, so they began contacting their missionary connections in order to find a way for me to get there. They organized two different trips for me to go on, and they both fell through. It was starting to look like it wasn't God's will for me to go after all, but there was one last option.

The couple from my church connected me with J.B. and Linda Godfrey. Dr. Godfrey was the Far East Director of Baptist International Missions Inc. at the time. The summer of 2010, I had the privilege of spending three weeks in Asia with them; two of those weeks were spent in the Philippines. At the time, I thought it was just a preview of what my life would be once I was old enough to be a missionary. However, looking back on it, I can see that God had a much bigger purpose for that trip.

I had never planned to go to West Coast Baptist College. In fact, I knew very little about West Coast. I had my heart set on going to a Bible college closer to my home in Tennessee, but my senior year of high school, I began to feel very unsettled about going to that particular college. I didn't understand why, but I knew that was not where I was supposed to go. Because I had been so fixated on one particular college, I didn't actually know much about other options. But in the summer of 2010, I had met Dr. Godfrey. At the time, Dr. Godfrey was a teacher in the missions department at West Coast. Because of that,

I did know a little bit about West Coast. I didn't have many other options to pursue, so I made a call to Dr. Godfrey. He encouraged me to visit West Coast, so a couple months later, my family did just that. By the end of our visit, my family had complete peace about sending me to West Coast. I thought it was for the purpose of preparing for the mission field, but once again, God had bigger plans.

As you already know, it was during my time at West Coast that God actually showed me my need for salvation. I know He could have done that no matter where I was, but He chose to do it at West Coast. It was also at West Coast that God changed my plans and turned my life upside down when He revealed that His will for my life was really to be a help meet to a man. Remember that day in Greek class when God whispered in my ear, *"This is not what I made you to do"?* There were some pretty crazy "coincidences" surrounding that event as well. The day God changed my plans was very shortly after the drop/add period for classes. At the time, I didn't understand why God would put me right in the middle of Greek class and then reveal that He didn't want me to be a Bible translator when it was too late for me to leave the class. However, "coincidentally," at the moment God whispered those words in my ear, the man for whom He was preparing me to be a help meet was sitting right behind me. It was in that Greek class that I would meet Steven.

A little girl who wanted to be a missionary? Coincidence? I think not.

Reader, absolutely nothing in your life is a coincidence. Every bit of your life is being orchestrated by God in order to fulfill His complete plan for your life. You may not have any idea right now what that is. Do you think Ruth had any idea that she would one day marry the man in whose field she was gleaning? Absolutely not! However, Ruth was faithful. She did what she knew she should do. And she trusted God to orchestrate the things she didn't know.

Trust God. He has a plan. *Nothing* in your life is a coincidence!

Psalm 37:23
The steps of a good man are ordered by the LORD:
and he delighteth in his way.

QUESTIONS FOR DISCUSSION

1. Looking back on your life, what are some things that looked like coincidences at the time but have turned out to be God's divine working?

2. Is there a circumstance in your life right now that doesn't seem to make sense? What is it? Do you believe that God could be using that circumstance somehow in the big picture of His plan for your life?

Chapter 4

GOD BLESSES
FAITHFULNESS

I will be faithful
When the end I cannot see.
I will be true
When those around me leave.
I will be strong
Even though I am weak.
I will be faithful,
For the Lord is my strength.

Being at the right place at the right time. I don't mean
by coincidence; I mean by intentional obedience to
God. Ruth was exactly where God wanted her to be,
and when we are exactly where God wants us to be,
He will always supply our needs. It's easy to get the
notion that God doesn't see our faithfulness. Does He
really see us when we get up early in the morning and

meditate on His Word before we start our day? Does He see us when we teach our little Sunday school class? Does He see us during the week being diligent in our jobs, or faithfully taking care of our homes and families? The answer to all of this is a resounding YES! God does see when we are faithful to Him, and He will always provide for the needs of those who are faithful.

God often chooses to pour out His blessings on us through the people He places in our lives. When we are faithful, God often isn't the only one who notices; the people God has placed in our lives will often notice as well. In the next verses, Boaz, our hero, finally walks into the story.

Ruth 2:4-7
And, behold, Boaz came from Bethlehem, and said unto the reapers, The LORD be with you. And they answered him, The LORD bless thee. Then said Boaz unto his servant that was set over the reapers, Whose damsel is this? And the servant that was set over the reapers answered and said, It is the Moabitish damsel that came back with Naomi out of the country of Moab: And she said, I pray you, let me glean and gather after the reapers among the sheaves: so she came, and hath continued even from the morning until now, that she tarried a little in the house.

Of course we know that God noticed Ruth in her faithfulness to honor both her mother-in-law and Himself. But God wasn't the only one who noticed! The workers in Boaz's field had taken notice of her as well, and when Boaz came for a visit, they gave him a good report of her. Needless to say, Boaz was quite impressed with her work ethic and her kindness to her mother-in-law. It is in this moment that Boaz first speaks to Ruth.

> *Ruth 2:8-9*
> *Then said Boaz unto Ruth, Hearest thou not, my daughter? Go not to glean in another field, neither go from hence, but abide here fast by my maidens: Let thine eyes be on the field that they do reap, and go thou after them: have I not charged the young men that they shall not touch thee? and when thou art athirst, go unto the vessels, and drink of that which the young men have drawn.*

Ruth is absolutely overwhelmed by his kindness! It makes absolutely no sense to her. Not only is she a lowly gleaner, but she is also a stranger. A foreigner. Most would consider her to be "heathen." She doesn't understand why this wealthy Jewish man would insist that she continue to glean in his field. She doesn't understand why he would offer her protection from any who would be unkind to her. She doesn't understand why he would even offer her the clean water that was really there for the paid workers. So she asks him why, and Boaz gives a revealing answer.

Ruth 2:10-12
Then she fell on her face, and bowed herself to the ground, and said unto him, Why have I found grace in thine eyes, that thou shouldest take knowledge of me, seeing I am a stranger? And Boaz answered and said unto her, It hath fully been shewed me, all that thou hast done unto thy mother in law since the death of thine husband: and how thou hast left thy father and thy mother, and the land of thy nativity, and art come unto a people which thou knewest not heretofore. The LORD recompense thy work, and a full reward be given thee of the LORD God of Israel, under whose wings thou art come to trust.

Ruth had been faithful, and it had not gone unnoticed. God was choosing to use Boaz as a vessel to bless her faithfulness. At this point, Ruth had no idea how much of a blessing Boaz would turn out to be. All she knew was that he was providing for her in a way that she did not deserve, all because of her faithfulness. And she was learning that God was always good, regardless of the circumstances.

Jesus tells another story about faithfulness in the New Testament; you may remember the parable about the talents. A rich man is going on a journey to a far away country. While he is gone, he leaves three of his servants with varying sums of money in the form of "talents." To the first servant he leaves five talents, to the second he leaves two, and to the third he leaves one.

The first two servants invested their talents and made a profit. However, the third servant buried his talent in the ground. After some time, the rich man returned, and desired to know what had been done with the talents he left with his servants. The first two servants showed him how they had invested the talents he had given them and doubled his money. His response to both of these servants was similar.

Matthew 25:23
His lord said unto him, Well done, good and faithful servant; thou hast been faithful over a few things, I will make thee ruler over many things: enter thou into the joy of thy lord.

Because these men had been faithful with what they had been given, their master gave them even greater opportunities. The third servant who had buried his talent? He tried to explain why he hadn't made use of his talent. He made excuses about his fear of not being able to do enough with it. The master's response to him was quite different than his response to the other two servants. He rebukes the servant and tells him that he should have invested his talent like the others had. Then, he commands that the foolish servant's talent should be taken away and given to the servant who had ten talents. His next statement is one that we can all learn something from.

Matthew 25:29
For unto every one that hath shall be given, and
he shall have abundance: but from him that hath
not shall be taken away even that which he hath.

To those who are faithful with what they have been given, God will give them more. To those who have not been faithful with what they already have, God will take away what they have. In the parable of the talents, this was in a monetary sense. In the life of Ruth, she was blessed for her faithfulness with greater opportunities. There are countless ways that God will bless us when we are faithful with what He has already given us.

Have you ever received a blessing because of faithfulness in your life? I know I have. There are quite a few stories I could tell you about God blessing me in a big way because of a little faithfulness, but perhaps one way I have seen this principle play out in my life time and time again is in my writing.

As I have mentioned before, I have always loved to write. Most of the time it has come relatively easily for me. However, there have been times that I have struggled to write anything. Some of those times have even been recently. There is one thing that these times of "writer's block" have certainly had in common: I was not using my writing in the way God wanted me to at the time. I could tell you several stories of times this has happened, but I will tell you the most recent story.

One area of writing that is a little more out of my comfort zone is song writing. However, over the last few years, God has allowed me to write several songs. I don't have a lot of musical ability, but God has allowed me to work with several musicians who have created piano arrangements for my songs after they listened to me sing the melody. God has recently been working in my heart to find different ways to use my writing to point others to Him. One way I believe He has called me to do that is in the writing of this book; another way is through singing the songs He allows me to write in my church.

That's the tricky part for me. I don't particularly enjoy singing in front of people. I don't mind public speaking, but something about singing somehow makes all the moisture disappear from my mouth and reappear in the form of sweaty palms. I'm a writer, not a singer, but singing is one of the means through which I can be faithful to share the things God has allowed me to write. After singing one of my songs in church about a year ago, I began to resist singing any others. It was honestly too terrifying of an experience! I didn't want to have to go through that again!

But my writing began to suffer. I wasn't writing new songs. Even the writing of this book began to suffer. I never really connected the two, but looking back now, I can see the clear connection.

A few months ago, I decided to muster up the courage to sing in church once again. It was still terrifying, but I decided I wasn't going to let that stop me from sharing the songs God had given to me. I quickly made plans to sing a third time. God saw that I was finally being faithful with what He had given me. And He quickly blessed me with more.

I started to write again. I continued the writing of this book, I wrote a new song, and I was even able to write a poem for the first time in over two years. God gave me the opportunity to write the Easter play for our church this year, and I am currently in the process of writing a Christmas play. God will not bless you with more if you are not faithful to do what He has called you to do with what He has already given you. In contrast, when you are faithful with what God has given you, the possibilities of how He will continue to bless you are truly endless.

Learning about how God blesses faithfulness would be useless if we failed to learn the proper response to His blessings. When God blesses us for our faithfulness to Him, the flesh often desires to respond with pride. Perhaps you're thinking, "Oh, I could never be prideful over my accomplishments! I'm so humble!" Be careful; false humility is just another manifestation of pride. When God uses the hand of Boaz to bless Ruth for her faithfulness, she shows us the correct response to these types of blessings.

Ruth 2:13-14
Then she said, Let me find favour in thy sight, my lord; for that thou hast comforted me, and for that thou hast spoken friendly unto thine hand-maid, though I be not like unto one of thine hand-maidens. And Boaz said unto her, At mealtime come thou hither, and eat of the bread, and dip thy morsel in the vinegar. And she sat beside the reapers: and he reached her parched corn, and she did eat, and was sufficed, and left.

The proper response to God's blessings is always receiving the blessing in thankfulness. We see in Ruth a grateful, humble spirit for the blessings she is receiving. She doesn't develop a sense of pride; she simply and humbly partakes of the blessings that God has provided for her through the hand of Boaz. She also doesn't put on a false show of humility by refusing the generosity of Boaz. She simply receives, and she does so with the correct spirit. Let's not forget to do the same when God blesses us greatly for our little faithfulness.

QUESTIONS FOR DISCUSSION

1. Has there ever been a time in your life when you received a blessing because of your faithfulness?

2. Has there ever been a time in your life that you believe God withheld His blessings because of your lack of faithfulness?

3. What are a few ways you could show more faithfulness in the things God has called you to do right now (at home, at church, at work, etc.)?

Chapter 5

HANDFULS OF PURPOSE

God always seems to give
Exceeding abundantly above.
I'll declare while I live:
How great is His love!

We've already learned that if we are faithful to God, He will provide for our needs. That should always be enough for us!

> *1 Timothy 6:8*
> *And having food and raiment let us be there-with content.*

If we have our basic needs met, we can be completely content. However, God often gives us even more than what we need for survival. We see that clearly in Ruth's story.

Ruth 2:15-17
And when she was risen up to glean, Boaz com-
manded his young men, saying, Let her glean even
among the sheaves, and reproach her not: And let
fall also some of the handfuls of purpose for her,
and leave them, that she may glean them, and
rebuke her not. So she gleaned in the field until
even, and beat out that she had gleaned: and it
was about an ephah of barley.

Not only did God provide for Ruth's basic needs of food and water, but He also provided food above and beyond what she needed to survive. A tenth part of an ephah was enough food for one person for one day. In one day, Ruth gathered ten times that much! That meant that in one day, she had gathered enough food for both Naomi and herself to eat for five days. Talk about a good day's work!

Has God ever gone above and beyond in His provision for you? The Bible tells us He is able to do so!

Ephesians 3:20
Now unto him that is able to do exceeding abun-
dantly above all that we ask or think, according to
the power that worketh in us,

I know God has done "exceeding abundantly above" all that I asked or thought on many occasions. The first occasion that comes to mind is the job that God provided me with right after college.

While I was in college, I was blessed to be able to spend summers and Christmas breaks at home with my family. During that time, God provided me with two part time jobs that were a wonderful blessing in helping me pay for college. Immediately after graduation, I returned to both of those jobs, with the intention of keeping them through the duration of my eight month engagement to Steven. However, it soon became apparent that the well of provision that those jobs had been was quickly drying up.

I was given fewer and fewer hours. I was spending five hours a week on the road, driving between the two jobs. I would have long gaps of time in the afternoon, sometimes as long as five hours, between the jobs. I was quickly becoming burnt out. And of course, with fewer hours came smaller paychecks. I was doing my best to save money to help Steven and myself to be able to have a strong start as a young couple in ministry. It became clear that if I were going to be able to achieve that goal, God would have to provide me with another job.

I didn't just sit around and wait for a job to come to me, as that approach rarely, if ever, secures a job. I started searching online for jobs I was qualified for, mainly in childcare or in a secretarial field. I spent as much time as I could filling out applications, but it seemed that I would never get a call for an interview. If I heard back from a potential employer, it was usually just to tell me they had selected someone else for the job. Then finally, one day, the call came.

I had applied for a front desk position at a local gym, and they wanted me to come in for an interview! It was so clear that God's hand was in this job opportunity. I would be able to have as many hours as I needed, and it was only a mile from my house. Spending less time traveling to work would provide more time to spend with my family. God was taking care of every detail.

At the interview, I found out it wasn't just a front desk position; my job would include some shifts at the front desk, and some shifts in childcare. I would be able to do both of the things I enjoyed doing! That was the first of many handfuls of purpose God gave me through that job. As the months went on, God continued to bless me through that job, and, in turn, allowed me to be a blessing to others. Ruth was a very wise woman in that when God blessed her, she was quick to pour out His blessing on others.

> *Ruth 2:18-22*
> *And she took it up, and went into the city: and her mother in law saw what she had gleaned: and she brought forth, and gave to her that she had reserved after she was sufficed. And her mother in law said unto her, Where hast thou gleaned to day? and where wroughtest thou? blessed be he that did take knowledge of thee. And she shewed*

her mother in law with whom she had wrought, and said, The man's name with whom I wrought to day is Boaz. And Naomi said unto her daughter in law, Blessed be he of the LORD, who hath not left off his kindness to the living and to the dead. And Naomi said unto her, The man is near of kin unto us, one of our next kinsmen. And Ruth the Moabitess said, He said unto me also, Thou shalt keep fast by my young men, until they have ended all my harvest. And Naomi said unto Ruth her daughter in law, It is good, my daughter, that thou go out with his maidens, that they meet thee not in any other field.

Ruth's blessing for working in the field of Boaz started off as "handfuls of purpose" in the form of food above and beyond that which she would have been able to normally glean. However, Ruth had no idea how many more "handfuls of purpose" working in the field of Boaz would provide. She had no idea that he was a near kinsman. She had no idea that he was the one who would be able to marry her and give her children. She was just doing what God had given her to do next. When we are following the Lord, we often find that He has something bigger in store for us as a result of our obedience than we could have ever imagined.

One "handful of purpose" that I received as a result of my job at the gym was a very flexible schedule.

If I needed time off for anything, I could have it. God gave me a wonderfully understanding boss who was always excited for me to be able to take time off to visit my fiancé or spend time with my family. She really believed that family time was the most important thing. When I first started that job, I didn't realize what a handful of purpose that would end up being.

On the morning of October 7, 2016, I was at work when I received a phone call that would change my life. My mom was out of town taking her parents to see relatives, and I knew she would never call me at work unless it was an emergency.

"Michelle, daddy was in an accident at work and hurt his hand. It looks like he may lose his thumb. I'll let you know when I find out what hospital they're taking him to so you can go be with him."

From what I was told, I had no idea how much that day would change my life. I had no idea how serious the situation really was. Actually, my mom had no idea how serious the situation was either. She was just relaying the information she had received from dad's co-worker over the phone.

When I arrived at the hospital, I found that dad's injuries were actually quite serious. A large container of chlorine dioxide had exploded while he had his right hand directly over the container. Yes, part of his thumb was gone, but that was just the beginning of it. His pinky was mostly detached, but they hoped to be able to save it. His ring finger was crushed. He had a broken wrist, shoulder, and collarbone. He had severe chemical burns covering 40% of his body. All of this added up to a very critical situation. However, the most serious injury of them all was the injury to his lungs. By God's grace, his internal organs were undamaged from the impact of the explosion, but he did suffer severe injury to his lungs due to chemical inhalation. The decision was quickly made to intubate him, as his lungs would need immense assistance functioning as they healed. Also, the decision was made to airlift him to another hospital that had a burn unit that would be equipped to handle his burns. By that evening, we were all at the burn unit, 144 miles from home.

Over the next few days, many decisions had to be made. There was no promise that dad would live. My brother flew in from college to visit. We had no idea if this would be the last time we ever saw dad on earth. We prayed desperately for healing, trusting that God would do His will.

However, it was obvious that if dad survived, he would be in the hospital for a very long time. I knew I needed to be at the hospital during that time to help my parents, and 144 miles was a little too much for a commute to work. For me, family would always come before work. My boss had graciously given me those first couple days off, but I knew I would have to call her and immediately resign. There was no other way. However, when I made the phone call, I was absolutely shocked at the outcome.

Even though I had only been working at the gym for a little over three months, my boss offered to put me on medical leave for as long as we were out of town with dad at the hospital. What an amazing "handful of purpose"! So much greater than anything I had imagined God would give me when I first accepted that job.

As it turned out, God answered prayer above and beyond what we could have ever imagined. Not only did dad recover from his injuries, we were only in the hospital and inpatient rehab for a combined total of twenty-five days. The miracle of dad's quick healing absolutely amazed the doctors and nurses, but it was just a testament to how great our God is!

When we returned home, dad had a lot of outpatient physical therapy ahead of him. He wasn't able to drive yet, so he would need someone to take him to all of his appointments. My mom and I both made the decision to return to work when we got home so that we could regain a sense of normalcy as soon as possible. When I called my boss to put me back on the schedule, I requested a change of hours that would allow for either my mom or myself to be with dad at all times. My boss was more than willing to make that accommodation for us. For the next two months until I got married, I was able to be with dad to help him whenever mom was at work, and I was still able to keep my job. When I accepted the job at the gym, I thought the extent of God's provision was a full-time job so I could save money to help start my life of marriage and ministry. I had no idea that the real blessing would be a compassionate boss who dropped God's handfuls of purpose for me in the form of being able to make my family a priority. I can't imagine having that level of flexibility at any other job.

As God's timing is always perfect, just a couple weeks before I got married, dad was able to start driving on his own again and was even able to return to work. I finished my time working at the gym. My dad got to walk me down the aisle on my wedding day. God had provided. Just enough. Just on time.

Ruth had no idea just what God had in store for her. She was just doing what she was supposed to do. She was certainly thankful that the workers in the field were giving her extra grain. But how could she have ever known that she had chosen the field of the one who could redeem her?

What handfuls of purpose has God placed in your life as a result of your following Him? Maybe they seem small to you. Or maybe you do have a story of just how much God can bless obedience. Maybe you haven't seen those handfuls of purpose yet. But dear reader, have faith. Have patience. God always blesses those who follow Him.

QUESTIONS FOR DISCUSSION

1. Describe a time when God provided "exceeding abundantly above" all that you asked or thought. What were the "handfuls of purpose" that He provided in addition to your basic needs?

2. Have you ever felt that God has failed to provide for your needs? How did He come through in the end with "handfuls of purpose"?

3. What are you asking God for right now? If it seems like He isn't answering, do you think He could be preparing to do something greater than you could even imagine?

Chapter 6

THE END OF
WHEAT HARVEST

I'm doing right now
What God has called me to do
In faith that somehow
In the end He'll come through.

During my junior year of college, God taught me a lesson from the book of Ruth that really changed my life. Or should I say, this lesson really is changing my life, for I continue to need its truth each and every day. Although I have chosen to approach this book about Ruth by walking chronologically through Ruth's story, the lesson we come to now is actually the first lesson from Ruth that God used in my life.

In the few years since discovering this next verse, it has become one of my favorite Bible verses of all time.

Ruth 2:23
So she kept fast by the maidens of Boaz to glean
unto the end of barley harvest and of wheat har-
vest; and dwelt with her mother in law.

It seems like a very odd, random verse, doesn't it? So how did this come to be one of the most impactful verses in the Bible for me? God brought it to my attention in my daily devotions during a difficult season of waiting in my life. He had recently made it very clear to me that His plan for my life was to be a help meet to a man and to be a godly mother. He taught me that I needed to stop pursuing so many things that were for my own personal advancement and start opening myself to simply being a godly wife and mother.

This was a very difficult thing for me to submit to because at that point, there was definitely not a man in my life. I mean, God may not have realized this, but it's very hard to be a wife and mother without a husband. I'm kidding of course, but that's just about how I was acting. I thought that plan was absolutely crazy. After all, I had no control over becoming a wife and mother!

But that was the point. I needed to stop trying to control my own life, and start letting God write my story. When I finally submitted to God's calling, a very uncertain season of waiting started. I really just wanted God to let Prince Charming walk right into my life the very minute I surrendered! But that's not how life works. Life is filled with seasons of waiting.

This season was an uncomfortable one. It was a scary season. I had just crossed the halfway point of my college career, and all of a sudden God was completely changing my plans! This was the time I was supposed to have everything figured out, not the time I was supposed to start all over again from scratch! By faith, I started telling people what God was revealing to me about His plan for my future. I was really discouraged that most people did not receive it well. I suppose I can understand; it certainly did look like I was trying to find an easier route than I had originally planned. To most people, being a godly wife and mother probably seemed like a much easier path than being a Bible translator in the Philippines. But to me, it was a giant leap of faith and surrender. So how does Ruth 2:23 play into all this? How did this verse so dramatically change my outlook on life?

When I read this verse in the fall of my junior year of college, I realized there was a truth there that I had never noticed before. This verse is easy to skim over. It doesn't seem to have any profound truth; it's just a part of the narrative. What I failed to realize previously was this: time passed. Ruth had to wait. We breeze right past this verse and read on to see how Boaz becomes the knight in shining armor, the kinsman redeemer. But Ruth had to wait through the entirety of barley harvest and the entirety of wheat harvest before any of that took place. How long of a time was this? Probably about three or four months.

God's waiting periods are different for everyone, but the fact is that everyone goes through periods of waiting in life. What is it that you're waiting for right now? At the time I read this passage, I was waiting for God to bring the right man into my life. I had no idea how long that would take. Ruth had no idea how long it would take for God to bring a man into her life to rescue her from the social stigma of being a barren widow. However, during her time of waiting, Ruth didn't just sit around fretting and focusing on the future she desired; she simply did the menial task before her.

We are so apt to get into this endless cycle of keeping our focus on whatever the next thing may be. I had been a slave to this cycle in my own life. I was always focused on the next thing, whether that was being in high school and focused on getting to college, or being in college focused on getting to the mission field. Then when God called me to be a help meet, and I surrendered, I started to spend all my time preoccupied with the thought of marriage. The problem with this is, if we are always preoccupied with the future, we will accomplish very little of real significance in the present.

Just because a season of life is mundane doesn't mean it's not important. In fact, we don't know much about the life of Jesus before He started His ministry at the age of thirty. We know about His birth, and we know that at the age of twelve His parents accidentally left Him in Jerusalem and then later found Him in the temple listening to the religious leaders and asking them questions. Between the ages of twelve and thirty, there is only one verse that tells us what Jesus was doing.

> *Luke 2:52*
> *And Jesus increased in wisdom and stature, and in favour with God and man.*

Jesus simply had a long season of growth. This season actually made up the majority of His life; His public ministry only lasted for three years. We don't know exactly what He did during this growing season, but I imagine He spent more time in the temple. I'm sure He spent His time at home being a blessing to His family. And I would assume He spent a very good bit of time learning the trade of his earthly father, Joseph: the trade of carpentry. It's very probable that a majority of Jesus' time on earth was spent in the "ordinary" trade of a carpenter. But God was preparing Him all along.

What did Ruth do? She gleaned. The ever-unglamorous, menial labor for widows and strangers. The thing that God had provided for her to do right then and there. What did God have for me to do during my time of waiting? Finish my Bible college degree. I had no idea *how* God would ever have me use the things I learned or if He *would* ever have me use the things I learned. All I knew was that I was exactly where I was supposed to be, doing exactly what I was supposed to be doing. Bible college was my barley field and wheat field.

So what's the next big thing for you? Is it college? Is it a career? Is it marriage? Is it children? Is it waiting for the children to be out of the house? Is it retirement? Whatever it may be, don't let your life slip by while you're busy being preoccupied with the next big thing. Do the thing that God has set before you, even if it seems like a little thing to you. What is that for you? It could be going to school. It could be working your regular job, each and every day. Maybe it's being a homemaker. Maybe it's being a stay at home mom. Maybe it's homeschooling your children. It could be just about anything. You know what it is for you. It's the daily task to which you *know* God has called you. When you spend less time focused on what God has called you to in the future and more time actually doing what He has called you to today, you will live a much more satisfied life.

It was about a year from the time God taught me this truth until He allowed my relationship with Steven to begin, and then it was another fifteen months until we were married. I had no idea how long my wait would be, just like Ruth had no idea how long her time of waiting would be. She didn't know that the end of wheat harvest would signal a new beginning for her life. The time frame isn't important; what is important is that we're serving the Lord while we wait for Him to accomplish His will for our lives.

It would be so easy for me to fall right back into the cycle of keeping my focus on "the next big thing." If I had to name what that is for me right now, I would probably say it would be the arrival of our first child. I could be absolutely consumed with the thought of the day we get to bring a baby home. Instead, I have to choose every day to do the tasks that God has set in front of me, to glean in my barley fields and my wheat fields. What does that look like for me? Preparing meals for my husband. Keeping a clean house. Serving in the children's ministry at church. Writing plays for our church. Writing this book. Life is so much more enjoyable when you learn to find contentment in the season of life God has you in right now.

So, what are you waiting for? Get on to that wheat harvest!

QUESTIONS FOR DISCUSSION

1. What is "the next big thing" that you are waiting for in your life right now? How much time do you spend dwelling on that thing?

2. What are the everyday, ordinary, average tasks that God has set before you to accomplish in *this* season? How could you do a better job of making those things your focus?

3. Can you think back to a time when, after a season of doing "ordinary" tasks, God blessed you with something extraordinary? How can the memory of that season encourage you to continue "gleaning" in the "barley fields and wheat fields" of your life?

Chapter 7

WHO'S YOUR
MOTHER-IN-LAW?

A peaceful dwelling place
With God at its core
Giving mercy and grace
Will forever endure.

Who's your mother-in-law? I don't mean literally, for
I am well aware that many of my readers may not yet
be married. But who is the person that God has called
you to dwell with in this season of life, just as God
called Ruth to dwell with Naomi?

> *Ruth 2:23*
> *So she kept fast by the maidens of Boaz to glean*
> *unto the end of barley harvest and of wheat har-*
> *vest; and dwelt with her mother in law.*

For Ruth, the person with whom God called her

to dwell was her mother-in-law. I'm sure Ruth's original plan in life did not involve moving in with her mother-in-law. When Ruth married Mahlon, I'm sure her plan was to live out the rest of her days dwelling with him. I love my mother-in-law, but I would most certainly rather dwell with my husband! God had a different plan for Ruth, and Ruth accepted that plan willingly and joyfully. It's probably unlikely that God will call you to dwell with your mother-in-law, but God will most certainly call you to dwell with *someone* during each season of your life.

God puts certain people in our lives in certain seasons for very specific reasons. During my junior year of college, when I was living in a dorm, I can tell you that I was certainly dreaming of dwelling with my husband rather than in a dorm full of girls! But God taught me so many things during that season, including the art of being content with the people with whom I was dwelling.

In my junior year of college, choosing to enjoy life with roommates made my college experience so much better. That year, my roommates Victoria and Amanda became two of the best friends I have ever had. They were really like the sisters I never had. I have so many wonderful memories of long talks and lunches. I also have many memories of praying for my husband with those girls as God had started working in my heart about being a help meet during the season in which He called me to dwell with them. Choosing to enjoy being with the people God has placed in your life may not always be your first response, but it is the best response. If you are not content with the people God has placed in your life now, the temptation will always be there to be discontent your company.

Following my college graduation, I had another lesson in being content with the people with whom God had called me to dwell. These two people were actually lifelong friends of mine, but it certainly wasn't in my original plan to dwell with them again. These people were my parents.

Very few people have the goal of moving back in with their parents after college. In fact, a major goal for most people is to be able to get their own place after college. When I had written my own story in my mind, I saw myself going off to the mission field immediately following graduation, never turning back. I absolutely love my parents, but as a twenty-two year old woman, moving back in with them was a little difficult.

The way God had planned my story, my fiancé would have one more semester of college after I graduated. This left us with an eight month engagement, and left me with my best option being moving back in with my parents. I didn't ever really dread it, but there were certainly times I wished Steven could have graduated with me and we could have started our life together sooner.

With my move back into the nest came the challenge of finding balance in my role as an adult daughter living at home. This wasn't always easy, but my parents and I worked together to find that balance. Looking back, I really am thankful for the time God gave me to spend with them before I moved across the country. I also learned that God always allows us to dwell in specific places for specific reasons.

As I mentioned in a previous chapter, during my time at home with my parents my dad was in a serious accident. What if I had gotten married immediately after graduation? Or what if I had decided to move somewhere on my own? Or go back to college to further my education? I wouldn't have been there to help my parents in the many ways they needed me to. God, in His sovereignty, allowed dad's accident to happen in the only eight month window of time that I would have been able to help in the way that I did. With God, there are no mistakes.

God has called us to live lives of peace with those around us.

Romans 12:18
If it be possible, as much as lieth in you, live peaceably with all men.

Maybe it doesn't seem possible to live peaceably with those in your home right now. However, the key to peace in the home is who is at the center. If you place yourself in the center, you will fail to have peace; if you place God at the center, He will create peace in your home.

Psalm 127:1
Except the LORD build the house, they labour in vain that build it: except the LORD keep the city, the watchman waketh but in vain.

Who is it that God has called you to dwell with? It's possible that you're still a teenager and haven't left home yet. In this case, it's quite obvious that God has called you to dwell with your parents and siblings. Don't waste that time! Be a blessing to your family. The day will come soon enough that you won't be dwelling with them. If you waste this time now, you will one day wish you had been more of a blessing while you had such a wonderful opportunity.

You could be in college, living in a dorm or sharing a home with roommates in some other way. I certainly know how difficult it is learning to mesh with completely different personalities in a dorm setting. Some of you may be in a similar situation as I was, having no choice over who your roommates are. When you're assigned to live with someone, there are bound to be areas in which your personalities clash. After all, you didn't choose them as a roommate, and they didn't choose you as a roommate either! However, this is a wonderful time to learn how to show God's grace. Be the person who gives in first. Be a peacemaker. I know from experience that this isn't easy, and there will probably be times you fail. Keep trying! God wants you to succeed, and with practice you will be able to learn how to dwell peacefully with others.

It's possible that God has given you the unique calling of moving back in with your parents as an adult daughter. Learn to see this as more than a time of waiting; learn to see this as a ministry opportunity. Your parents have given so much for you, and are certainly giving even more for you in allowing you to come home as an adult daughter. This is a privilege! Find ways to be a blessing to your parents in return. Learning your role as an adult daughter may be hard, especially after spending so much of your life as a child under the complete authority of your parents. However, with God at the center, this can be a wonderful season of life.

Maybe you're married already and you're learning that dwelling with your husband isn't as easy as you thought it would be. Of course you love each other, but you're still two different people with completely different personalities learning to share a life together. In our world today, submission is one of the hardest lessons for women to learn. We are taught by society from a young age that the most important thing is to be independent; we don't need men in order to succeed! However, the Bible teaches that we are to submit to our husbands. If you are having this quiet, submissive spirit at home and your husband is following God's command to love you as Christ loved the church, you will be able to learn to dwell peacefully together.

Perhaps you have children at home. Maybe you're even homeschooling your children. This is a new season of life with new people with whom you must learn to dwell. Sometimes these little people may be quite demanding! They take so much of your energy and time; maybe they're the most difficult people you've had to dwell with yet. However, during this season of life, it is important to remember that these little people are a gift from God. You have the privilege of having the greatest impact on their life. You have the opportunity to guide them to become godly young people. And you can learn to dwell with them.

Maybe your children are grown and you're learning to dwell with your husband all over again. For years there have been little ones in the house, but now it's the two of you once more. My parents are entering this season right now as new "empty nesters." This doesn't have to be a bad time; this can be a wonderful time of new, fun memories that you may not have been able to make while you had children at home. Learn to dwell with your husband, all over again.

Perhaps you do live on your own. The people with

whom you must dwell are not limited to the people in your home; maybe you have coworkers who are difficult to dwell with. You can choose to love them. You can choose to show Christ to them. The reality is, they won't be in your life forever; use the time you have with them to be a blessing. If they see a difference in your life, that may be just the thing they need to point them to Christ.

So, with whom has God called you to dwell? It doesn't matter how difficult of a person they are. It doesn't matter if you just don't get along with them. God has put them in your life for a very specific reason. What is that reason? You may not find out until you start trying to dwell peacefully with them. God puts us in other people's lives to be a blessing. You won't be a blessing just by focusing on yourself and hoping for the best. Actively look for ways to be a blessing. If you really want to be a blessing, God will show you what to do. He always helps those who are seeking to be pleasing to Him.

So let me ask once more, who's your mother-in-law?

QUESTIONS FOR DISCUSSION

1. With whom has God called you to dwell in this season of your life?

2. What are some ways you can actively create a peaceful environment in which to dwell with those people?

3. Think of some of the people you have been called to dwell with in the past. How has keeping God at the center of your home created a peaceful environment? How has rejecting God as the center of your home created an environment of contention?

Chapter 8

NO "PLAN B"

*I'll follow God's will
With no turning back;
I know He loves me still,
And His provision never lacks.*

Following God's will is easy, isn't it? After all, if for some reason it doesn't work out, there's always your "Plan B." You could easily just continue your education post-graduation. That job you have now? Well, they would take you back if following God's will doesn't work out. In fact, you just so happen to know of someone who would offer you a job at any time if they knew you had a need! So you decide to try this whole "God's will" thing for a little while, and if it doesn't work out, you can always turn to your "Plan B." The problem with this is, it eliminates faith from the equation.

Hebrews 11:6
But without faith it is impossible to please him:
for he that cometh to God must believe that he is,
and that he is a rewarder of them that diligent-
ly seek him.

If you have another plan as a safety net "just in case," you really don't have faith that God will provide for what He has called you to do. There is no way you can please God without faith, even if you are trying to follow the calling He has placed on your life.

Finally, the day came that God revealed the next step He had planned for Ruth's life.

Ruth 3:1-4
Then Naomi her mother in law said unto her, My daughter, shall I not seek rest for thee, that it may be well with thee? And now is not Boaz of our kindred, with whose maidens thou wast? Behold, he winnoweth barley to night in the threshingfloor. Wash thyself therefore, and anoint thee, and put thy raiment upon thee, and get thee down to the floor: but make not thyself known unto the man, until he shall have done eating and drinking. And it shall be, when he lieth down, that thou shalt mark the place where he shall lie, and thou shalt go in, and uncover his feet, and lay thee down; and he will tell thee what thou shalt do.

God had actually made another provision for Ruth

before she was even born. We see this provision described in the law.

> *Deuteronomy 25:5*
> *If brethren dwell together, and one of them die, and have no child, the wife of the dead shall not marry without unto a stranger: her husband's brother shall go in unto her, and take her to him to wife, and perform the duty of an husband's brother unto her.*

God knew that there would be young, barren widows. God knew that in the cultural context of Israel, these women would become outcasts. God knew these women would need someone to provide for them. So God, in His law, made a provision for these women whom He loved so much. If a woman's husband died, that man's brother would be bound by law to marry his brother's widow. Mahlon didn't have any living brothers, so this task fell to whomever was the next nearest kinsman. As far as Naomi knew, this "just so happened" to be Boaz, the man in whose fields Ruth had been gleaning all that time. Of course, we don't believe in "just so happened"; we believe God had a plan all along.

Ruth more than likely wasn't familiar with all the Jewish laws; after all, she was a Moabitess, a stranger in the land. However, her loving mother-in-law, Naomi, with whom she had been dwelling, knew all about the laws. Ruth also didn't know who any of her husband's family were. She had met her husband in her own native land, and had only been in her husband's home land for a short time. But Naomi knew all of hers and her husband's kindred. She knew who Boaz was. And she was very eager to share this information with her faithful daughter-in-law.

When Ruth received the knowledge of this "nearest kinsman" thing, she had a couple of options. First of all, she could have refused to follow the plan Naomi had set out for her. Ruth could have come up with her own plan to provide for herself. Perhaps she could have formulated a plan that included fewer risks. This is a temptation we too often face in our own lives, whether we realize it or not. I have faced this temptation in my life just in the process of writing this book.

When my husband and I first moved to Utah, God made it very clear to me that writing this book was the next step in His plan for my life. As soon as we finished unpacking, I started my writing with a passion in my heart to use my words and the lessons God had taught me to be an encouragement to others. I was making quick progress, but after just a few months, I was gripped with fear that brought my progress to a halt.

Sharing my story and the lessons that God has taught me in life involves a measure of risk. I'm usually a very shy, quiet person. I really have to put forth a great effort to get to know people. Making my story available to be read by anyone who desired to do so began to scare me. So I started to fill my schedule with less important things, things that occupied my time and gave me an excuse not to write.

Don't misunderstand me here; I wasn't filling my life with bad things. I was babysitting, I was helping with our family income by opening an online shop, and I was saying "yes" to everything anyone from our church asked me to help with. I filled my life with good things, but I was still less than fulfilled because I wasn't doing the thing I knew God had called me to do in that season. I wasn't using the gift for writing that God had given me to share my story and be a blessing to others. I'm glad God is always so patient with me. His invitation to use my writing for Him was still open when I got past my fears and surrendered all over again. Sometimes we have to learn to say no to the "good" things in life in order to make more time for the "best" things.

What if Ruth had chosen to fill her life with things that were less than God's best for her? What if she had chosen to just continue gleaning in the fields? That seems like it would be a relatively safe option, and it would be an honest way to provide for herself and for Naomi. There would have been nothing inherently wrong with continuing to be a gleaner, but it would have been less than what God had for her. It would have never fulfilled her in life.

Ruth's next option would be to follow the plan Naomi had set out for her, but still have thoughts in the back of her mind of the things she could do "if it didn't work out." I remember the days of temptation to make a "Plan B" very clearly.

When I realized God was calling me to be a wife and mother, I was initially very excited. Quite a few people were very excited for me. However, there were others who didn't quite understand how this could be since there was no man in my life. Nobody was un-kind, but several people made their own suggestions of things they felt were "more practical."

"You know, you could be a teacher and work with children. That way you get to work with children wheth-er or not you ever have any of your own."

"There are lots of orphanages in Africa that need help. That would be a good way for you to be able to invest in children."

"You want to be a wife and mother? That's great! But what else are you going to do? That can't be all there is to it."

These were actual responses I received. I was sometimes discouraged by these responses, and sometimes I was tempted to make my own "Plan B," in case things didn't work out. But I became very con-victed over this. I realized that I was cutting faith out of the equation. I had a choice to make. And I chose to believe that God would provide for what He had called me to do, in His timing.

Ruth made the same choice. She chose to follow Naomi's instructions with complete abandonment, believing God had provided a husband and a future for her.

> *Ruth 3:5*
> *And she said unto her, All that thou sayest unto me I will do.*

She didn't question. She didn't say, "Yes, but..." She simply agreed to the plan Naomi had laid out for her. The plan that God had laid out for women who He knew would be in her very situation. The next few verses tell us exactly what happened when Ruth acted in obedience.

> *Ruth 3:6-11*
> *And she went down unto the floor, and did according to all that her mother in law bade her. And when Boaz had eaten and drunk, and his heart was merry, he went to lie down at the end of the heap of corn: and she came softly, and uncovered his feet, and laid her down. And it came to pass at midnight, that the man was afraid, and turned himself: and, behold, a woman lay at his feet. And he said, Who art thou? And she answered, I am Ruth thine handmaid: spread therefore thy skirt over thine handmaid; for thou art a*

near kinsman. And he said, Blessed be thou of the LORD, my daughter: for thou hast shewed more kindness in the latter end than at the beginning, inasmuch as thou followedst not young men, whether poor or rich. And now, my daughter, fear not; I will do to thee all that thou requirest: for all the city of my people doth know that thou art a virtuous woman.

Even if she didn't understand it, Ruth followed Naomi's plan exactly in order to reveal to Boaz who she was. Ruth may have wondered at times if Boaz would take her in or if he would reject her; after all, even though she was the widow of his near kinsman, she was still a stranger in the land. But she didn't make a "Plan B." She didn't compromise. She followed God's plan. And as we know, the response she received from Boaz was favorable. He was indeed willing to perform the duty of the kinsman redeemer.

What's your "Plan B"? Throw it out. God's plan is always better.

QUESTIONS FOR DISCUSSION

1. Do you have a "Plan B" in case God's will doesn't work out? What is it? What steps do you need to take to daily refuse the thing that is less than God's best?

2. Are you doing something right now that isn't wrong, but it isn't what God wants you to be doing right now? What is it? What steps can you take today to say no to the "good" things so you have more time for the "best" things?

3. Has there been a time in your life when you followed God's will without making a "Plan B"? How did God bless your faith? How can the memory of that time encourage you to continue following God's will today?

Chapter 9

GOD'S DELAYS

God may delay,
But He will not deny;
Where He has called,
He will always provide.

What if God has already revealed to you what His next step for your life is, but all the doors seem to be closing? That can't be right! If it's God's will, everything should just fall into place with no problems whatsoever. Have you ever heard the expression, "God's delays are not God's denials"? This is absolutely true. Sometimes even when we are trying to follow God's will, there are delays on our journey. This doesn't mean we're no longer on the right track; it just means that God's plan is taking a little longer to unfold than our finite minds think is reasonable. However, God in His infinite wisdom knows exactly what is going to happen next. He will allow His will for us to unfold in His perfect timing. In the next segment of Ruth's story, we see a delay. This delay may seem like a bump in the road to us, but it was all part of God's perfect plan for Ruth's life.

> *Ruth 3:12-13*
> *And now it is true that I am thy near kinsman: howbeit there is a kinsman nearer than I. Tarry this night, and it shall be in the morning, that if he will perform unto thee the part of a kinsman, well; let him do the kinsman's part: but if he will not do the part of a kinsman to thee, then will I do the part of a kinsman to thee, as the LORD liveth: lie down until the morning.*

Plot twist! Boaz may have been a near kinsman, but he wasn't the nearest kinsman. Just when everything seemed to be going just right, we find that there's a chance that Boaz, the knight in shining armor, may not be able to come to Ruth's rescue after all. He couldn't give a definitive answer of whether or not he would be able to redeem Ruth until he had spoken with the nearer kinsman the next day. I can't imagine that Ruth got much sleep that night.

> *Ruth 3:14*
> *And she lay at his feet until the morning: and she rose up before one could know another.*

She lay at his feet. She may or may not have slept,

but if Ruth was anything like I am, she was a bit anxious all night. I like to have the solution to the problem now. I want to know how the story ends! When I know God has something exciting in store for me, I want to jump ahead and experience it right away. However, sometimes God allows delays so He can grow our faith. Thankfully, Ruth only had to wait until the next day to find out what the conclusion would be. We may find, at times, that God allows our delays to be a bit longer. And sometimes we don't even know when the delay will be over. In recent years, I watched my dad go through a delay from God that seemed like it would never end.

My dad is the perfect picture of the hard-working American. He applied for his first job the day he turned sixteen, and he's been working ever since. He's done everything in his power to make sure his family was taken care of, and his performance on the job has always been excellent. As Christians, we know that no matter what our job is, we're not working for man; we're working for the Lord. Dad's co-workers have always known he is a Christian, and his work ethic shows it.

Dad has worked several different jobs over the years, but most of them have been in the food manufacturing industry. At times he has had to change jobs for one reason or another, but God has *always* provided. Several years ago, he was in a situation where he needed a new job because the company for which he was working was closing their location in our hometown. Relocating wasn't an option at the time, so dad immediately started the job hunt. God provided very quickly, and dad didn't even have a gap of unemployment between jobs. The job God provided wasn't really perfect in our eyes, but it was good. And we were thankful.

Over time, dad's new job started requiring him to work an occasional Sunday. This didn't cause too much of a problem at first, but "occasionally" quickly turned into "more often than not." This was extremely difficult for my dad, as he has always placed a high priority on church for our family. Sometimes there would seem to be an opening for a job in his field, but it seemed like God closed every seemingly open door. We didn't understand why God would allow such a delay. Little did we know, the biggest bump in the road was yet to come.

This is the part in the story when dad's accident takes place. God gave him a miraculous recovery, but returning to work was extremely difficult. Even though my dad was in a management position, his job was still very demanding physically. Before the accident, that wasn't a problem. However, with dad's new limited use of his right hand, his job became very taxing physically. It seemed like God was running late to move the mountain. However, that is when we all had to remember a lesson God taught my mom years before, when dad was going through another difficult work situation. We didn't understand why God wasn't fixing it!

Do you remember the story of Abraham and Isaac on Mount Moriah in Genesis 22? God had commanded Abraham to take his son, the son of the promise, to the mountains in Moriah and offer him as a burnt sacrifice. To us, this makes absolutely no sense! But Abraham didn't question God. He trusted God wholeheartedly; he believed God would either provide a sacrifice in Isaac's place, or He would raise Isaac from the dead. As difficult as it must have been, Abraham obeyed God and took Isaac to the top of the mountain. He prepared Isaac to be the sacrifice, and Isaac was willing to submit, both in obedience to God and to his father. When we get to verse 10 of the chapter, it looks like it's too late.

Genesis 22:10
And Abraham stretched forth his hand, and took the knife to slay his son.

This would surely be the end for Isaac! However, in the very next verse, the angel of the Lord calls out to Abraham to stop him. At this point in the story, the angel brings Abraham's attention to a ram that was caught in a nearby thicket. This was to be the sacrifice to replace Isaac.

There's something I want you to notice here that is not explicitly mentioned in this passage, but I believe can easily be inferred: *the ram was not in the thicket until Abraham had raised the knife.* Why do I believe this? If a ram was caught in a thicket by his horns, do you think that ram would be silent? Absolutely not! Abraham would have surely heard the ram if it had been there all along! So why did God wait so long to put the ram, the provision for Abraham's need, in the thicket? We see the answer in the latter part of verse 12.

Genesis 22:12
...for now I know that thou fearest God, seeing thou hast not withheld thy son, thine only son from me.

The purpose of the whole ordeal was to prove Abraham's faith. Why would we think that God wouldn't allow things to happen in our lives to prove our faith as well? When my family goes through faith trying times like these, we remember that sometimes, God doesn't put the ram in the thicket until the knife has been raised. If the provision isn't there, the knife must not have been raised yet. When the crucial moment finally comes, God will always provide.

After the accident, dad had been back at his job for a few months when he heard of a potential opportunity in his field. This job would be less hands-on, and the hours would be less physically exhausting. The odds weren't exactly in my dad's favor to get the job, but after a few more months of lots of interviews and even more prayer, he was hired. And he hasn't had to work a Sunday ever since.

I'm sure Ruth was ready for her happily ever after, but even in the midst of God's seemingly perfect provision, there was a delay. In faith, Ruth continued to follow the instructions of the people God had placed in her life for guidance. She accepted God's delays with grace.

Maybe you're going through a delay of your own right now. Maybe it's taking longer than you thought it would to meet the man God would have you to marry. Maybe you're struggling to have children. Maybe you believe God is leading you to a career change, but it doesn't seem like He's opening the doors. The possibilities of what you are waiting for are endless. I know it's easy to get discouraged, but don't allow God's delays to make you angry with Him. Just keep trusting that His plan for you is good, and allow Him to use whatever situation you are in to build your faith. He will provide a ram, but not until the knife is raised.

QUESTIONS FOR DISCUSSION

1. Describe a time in your life when God provided for you, even when it seemed like He would delay until it was too late.

2. What provision are you waiting for right now? Does it seem like God is delaying? What might God be teaching you during this delay?

3. Is there a Bible verse that you could choose as a reminder that God will always provide, right on time?

Chapter 10

SIT STILL

When life slows down
And all is quiet and still,
It is then I have found
My God to be most real.

Do you ever have a hard time sitting still? Being still usually goes against the flow of our culture. Sometimes it even goes against the flow of our Christian culture! Our world idolizes always being busy, and in many cases, the church has often adopted this philosophy as well. Please don't misunderstand me; there is definitely a time to take action, like we discussed earlier. Always be sensitive to what God calls you to do. Ruth was sensitive to God's call to action when she was gleaning in the fields, but she was also sensitive to His call when that calling was to sit still.

Ruth 3:15-18

And he said, Let it not be known that a woman came into the floor. Also he said, Bring the vail that thou hast upon thee, and hold it. And when she held it, he measured six measures of barley, and laid it on her: and she went into the city. And when she came to her mother in law, she said, Who art thou, my daughter? And she told her all that the man had done to her. And she said, These six measures of barley gave he me; for he said to me, Go not empty unto thy mother in law. Then said she, Sit still, my daughter, until thou know how the matter will fall: for the man will not be in rest, until he have finished the thing this day.

It would appear as though we have reached the climax of our story; Boaz has agreed to be the kinsman redeemer, provided that the nearer kinsman doesn't want to take on the responsibility. Of course Boaz is going to be the redeemer! This is a real life fairytale, written down for time and posterity! As we know, the story continues to move forward, and they live happily ever after. But Ruth doesn't know that; she isn't able to read her own story in a book. For her, the story is still unfolding. And even though it seems she has already gone through so much waiting, she is presented with a call to wait some more. Whereas her first time of waiting was an active waiting involving reaping in the barley and wheat harvests, this is a passive waiting. She is simply called to sit still. Although waiting actively is difficult, I truly believe waiting passively is much more difficult. It is in the passive waiting that we truly deepen our relationship with God.

Psalm 46:10
Be still, and know that I am God: I will be exalted among the heathen, I will be exalted in the earth.

Right before God does something really big, He often calls us to a time of stillness. For some of us, that stillness can be more difficult than for others. Regardless, it is in the stillness that God teaches us who He is and prepares us for the big, wonderful things that are to come.

My parents and I had a time of stillness during my dad's hospital stay after his accident. I can truly say that during that time, I came to know God in a closer way than I ever had before. I think I can attribute that to a lot of time "sitting still."

To say that our lives slowed down during dad's hospital stay would be an understatement; our lives came to a screeching halt. My mom, my dad, and I had been living in the same house, but we were in an exceptionally busy season of life in which we didn't get to spend a lot of time with all three of us together. We were all working full time jobs, and my dad's job was more than full time. My younger brother was away at college; the days of "us four" time had drawn to a close. In fact, in this busy season of our lives, my mom was actually out of town for the weekend helping her parents at the time of dad's accident. I was at my job. But the moment that phone call came, our lives synced up instantly. My mom and I were both at the emergency room as soon as we possibly could be, and from that moment on, we hardly left dad's side until we got to take him home.

Dad was airlifted from our local emergency room to a burn unit 144 miles from home, and mom and I followed in our van. We didn't know exactly how long we would be at the hospital with dad, but we packed clothes for a few days before leaving. We never could have imagined the road that was ahead of us.

When we arrived at the hospital, we were told that dad's injuries were much worse than we had originally thought. If he recovered at all, he would be in the hospital for weeks, possibly months. As I mentioned in a previous chapter, it was never a question of whether or not mom and I would stay with him; we took an indefinite leave from our respective jobs, I packed more clothes during a necessary trip home a few days later, and we prepared for the long haul. We spent the first couple of nights on the floor of the hospital waiting room, but we were soon able to move into a hotel room. We may have slept at the hotel room, but we lived at the hospital. We were there every day before visiting hours began to hear the doctors' reports from the night before, and we were there until the last possible minute each evening. We ate all our meals there. We barely spent any time outside dad's room in the intensive care unit. If I could describe our time there in one word, it would be this: still.

We didn't watch television. Even though I had brought several books to read, I only read a few pages during our entire stay. We sang a lot of songs, but other than that, our time was very quiet and very still. Doctors came in and out all day long, and we had a few visitors here and there, including a very special visit with my brother for a couple of days. However, for the majority of our time, it was just the three of us in that quiet room. Actually, it was the four of us; God was very obviously in that intensive care unit room. Remembering that time makes me think of another story from the Bible.

Do you remember the story about the three Hebrew children who were cast into the fiery furnace in Babylon because they refused to worship anyone other than the one true God? What King Nebuchadnezzar said he saw after they had been cast into the furnace is truly remarkable.

Daniel 3:24-25
Then Nebuchadnezzar the king was astonied, and rose up in haste, and spake, and said unto his counsellers, Did not we cast three men bound into

the midst of the fire? They answered and said unto
the king, True, O king. He answered and said, Lo,
I see four men loose, walking in the midst of the
fire, and they have no hurt; and the form of the
fourth is like the Son of God.

Nebuchadnezzar saw a Fourth Man walking in the fiery furnace; that Fourth Man was Jesus, who *is* God. Jesus was also the Fourth Man in our intensive care unit room. He was there the whole time we were there in our own fiery furnace. In fact, He was even there with dad at night when mom and I had to go back to the hotel to sleep. He was also in the hotel room with mom and me. The truth of the matter is, the Fourth Man is still with me in this very moment. But I don't think He's ever been more obviously real to me than He was in those days where we had nothing to do but sit still.

The days of sitting still came to an end even sooner than we had originally been told. As I have previously stated, after twenty-five days in the hospital and inpatient rehab, we were able to take dad home. Mom and I both went back to our jobs part time, arranging our schedules to make sure dad never had to be alone and always had someone to take him to physical therapy. Our time of truly sitting still had come to an end. But in a way, dad's time of sitting still had just begun.

I mentioned previously that my dad is a very hard working man. Sitting still is not in his vocabulary.

He's at work early, even when he doesn't have to be; his work ethic is one that I admire. But when we got home, he was far from ready to return to work. He no longer needed twenty-four hour medical care, but his body still had a lot of recovery to do. And he had a lot of sitting still to do.

I can't tell you everything that was going on in my dad's heart and mind during this time because it's not something that's come up in conversation, and I honestly have no desire to ask about it. I know what went on between God and my dad during those weeks must have been very personal. I know this just because of the things I observed. (Let this be a lesson, your kids really are watching you, no matter how old they are.)

I watched in the early days when my dad wasn't able to read due to the damage the chemicals had done to his eyes. I watched him as he sat in the living room listening to the Bible being read aloud or listening to uplifting Christian music. In fact, I didn't even have to watch in those days; I could hear what was going on from multiple rooms in the house. I could hear my dad singing to the Lord. And I could hear his tears as he allowed the Lord to work in his heart.

As God healed dad's eyes, I got to watch him sit on the couch with his open Bible, just like he had before our lives had been turned upside down. This makes me think of another verse in the book of Daniel.

Daniel 6:10

Now when Daniel knew that the writing was signed, he went into his house; and his windows being open in his chamber toward Jerusalem, he kneeled upon his knees three times a day, and prayed, and gave thanks before his God, as he did aforetime.

It may be easy to walk with God when everything is going well, but Daniel continued to walk with God even when things stopped going well. For Daniel, continuing to walk with God meant certain death (as far as anyone knew). For us, it may just be that it takes a deeper measure of faith to walk with God "after" the hard times have come than it took to walk with Him "before." But in those days at home with my dad, I saw him walk with God, just as he had before.

I can't tell you exactly what God did in my dad's life during those days, but there is one thing I can tell you for certain: my dad grew to know God in a greater way than he ever had before. Does this mean that he wasn't a strong believer before? Absolutely not! It doesn't matter how old you are or how long you have been a believer, we always need to grow in our walk with God. You should be concerned if you come to a point where you think you're finished growing. I'm glad I have a dad who allowed God to use a time of "sitting still" to deepen his knowledge of who God really is. I know when he returned to work three months after his accident he was equipped more than ever before for the daily battles he faced, simply because he knew God better through a time of sitting still.

If you're currently in a season of sitting still, I understand that it can be difficult. Maybe your season of sitting still has lasted longer than a few weeks or months; maybe you've been sitting still for years. Use this time to get to know God better. When the time of sitting still has come to its end, you will be thankful that you allowed God to use it in the way He intended.

QUESTIONS FOR DISCUSSION

1. Has there ever been a time in your life when God called you to "sit still"?

2. In what ways did you come to know God better during that time?

3. If you are in a time of "sitting still" right now, what are some practical ways you can use this time to grow in your relationship with the Lord?

Chapter 11

THE PROCESSES

I'll do things God's way
With no questions asked;
I trust Him each day
To give strength for the task.

I believe it is part of our sinful human nature that makes us so good at finding the easy way out. At a young age, we discover that there is a shortcut for most things. Sometimes this can be good and helpful; managing the time God has given us wisely and making the most of our days is a part of good stewardship. However, there are times that taking the shortcut is truly harmful in the long run. When God has prescribed a way in which He intends for something to be done, either through His Word or through the leading of the Holy Spirit in your life individually, trying to take the shortcut is disobedience. When we choose to disobey God by taking shortcuts, we miss out on the blessings He has for us in the journey. It is so important for us to learn not to try to jump ahead in God's plan for our lives. In the final chapter of the book of Ruth, Boaz is faced with the opportunity to "take a shortcut" that could have been very detrimental to his future with Ruth.

We know by now that Boaz loves Ruth and wants to marry her. However, the law states that she is to marry the *nearest* kinsman, not just a near kinsman. God was very specific in His law.

Deuteronomy 25:5
If brethren dwell together, and one of them die, and have no child, the wife of the dead shall not marry without unto a stranger: her husband's brother shall go in unto her, and take her to him to wife, and perform the duty of an husband's brother unto her.

If Ruth's husband's brother had still been living, it would have been his duty to marry her and have children with her. However, because Ruth's only brother-in-law had also passed away, this responsibility fell to whomever was the next nearest kinsman. As we learned a couple chapters ago, Boaz was a near kinsman, but he knew there was a nearer kinsman. He was faced with a choice; he could disobey God's law, take a shortcut, and just marry Ruth, or he could do the right thing and give the true nearest kinsman the opportunity to be the kinsman redeemer. Boaz loved Ruth, but he was a man who knew the value of doing things in the order God intended. While Ruth was busy "sitting still," Boaz immediately set forth to follow the process which God had laid out.

> *Ruth 4:1-4*
> *Then went Boaz up to the gate, and sat him down there: and, behold, the kinsman of whom Boaz spake came by; unto whom he said, Ho, such a one! turn aside, sit down here, And he turned aside, and sat down. And he took ten men of the elders of the city, and said, Sit ye down here. And they sat down. And he said unto the kinsman, Naomi, that is come again out of the country of Moab, selleth a parcel of land, which was our brother Elimelech's: and I thought to advertise thee, saying, Buy it before the inhabitants, and before the elders of my people. If thou wilt redeem it, redeem it: but if thou wilt not redeem it, then tell me, that I may know: for there is none to redeem it beside thee; and I am after thee. And he said, I will redeem it.*

Oh, did I forget to mention that accepting the role of the kinsman redeemer also included the opportunity of purchasing a piece of land from Naomi? That's because the book of Ruth doesn't mention this land up until this point in the story. Boaz simply loved

Ruth. He didn't care about the land that he could pur-
chase as the kinsman redeemer; he simply wanted to
marry the woman he loved. However, he knew that
the opportunity of gaining this parcel of land would
be an attractive prospect for this other kinsman, even
if he had no interest in marrying Ruth. Boaz, being
the honorable man that he was, did not try to make
the role of kinsman redeemer seem unattractive in
any way in order to make the potential outcome more
favorable for himself; he was honest, and he even presented the opportunity for increase in land at the very
beginning. Of course, the kinsman eagerly agreed to
redeem the land. But again, because Boaz was an honest man, he then made clear to the kinsman what the
rest of the deal entailed.

> Ruth 4:5-6
> Then said Boaz, What day thou buyest the field of
> the hand of Naomi, thou must buy it also of Ruth
> the Moabitess, the wife of the dead, to raise up the
> name of the dead upon his inheritance. And the
> kinsman said, I cannot redeem it for myself, lest I
> mar mine own inheritance: redeem thou my right
> to thyself; for I cannot redeem it.

When the kinsman hears "the rest of the story,"
he realizes that gaining this land won't be as advan-
tageous to himself as he originally thought. In fact,
he would be required to raise up children for Mahlon,

and the land would one day be theirs. The kinsman was concerned about what effect this would have on his own future; he wanted to raise up a name for himself. Because of this, he declined to redeem the land and marry Ruth. Once again, God had already laid out in the law what should take place in a situation such as this.

> *Deuteronomy 25:7-10*
> *And if the man like not to take his brother's wife, then let his brother's wife go up to the gate unto the elders, and say, My husband's brother refuseth to raise up unto his brother a name in Israel, he will not perform the duty of my husband's brother. Then the elders of his city shall call him, and speak unto him: and if he stand to it, and say, I like not to take her; then shall his brother's wife come unto him in the presence of the elders, and loose his shoe from off his foot, and spit in his face, and shall answer and say, So shall it be done unto that man that will not build up his brother's house. And his name shall be called in Israel, The house of him that hath his shoe loosed.*

Boaz had already gathered the elders; all that was left was the matter of the ceremony which God had prescribed for those who refuse to become the kinsman redeemer.

Ruth 4:7-11

Now this was the manner in former time in Israel concerning redeeming and concerning changing, for to confirm all things; a man plucked off his shoe, and gave it to his neighbor: and this was a testimony in Israel. Therefore the kinsman said unto Boaz, Buy it for thee. So he drew off his shoe. And Boaz said unto the elders, and unto all the people, Ye are witnesses this day, that I have bought all that was Elimelech's, and all that was Chilion's and Mahlon's, of the hand of Naomi. Moreover Ruth the Moabitess, the wife of Mahlon, have I purchased to be my wife, to raise up the name of the dead upon his inheritance, that the name of the dead be not cut off from among his brethren, and from the gate of his place: ye are witnesses this day. And all the people that were in the gate, and the elders, said, We are witnesses. The LORD make the woman that is come into thine house like Rachel and like Leah which two did build the house of Israel: and do thou worthily in Ephratah and be famous in Bethlehem: and let thy house be like the house of Pharez, whom Tamar bare unto Judah, of the seed which the LORD shall give thee of this young woman.

It seems that the only part of the process ordained by God that was omitted was spitting in the face of the kinsman who refused to redeem Ruth. Perhaps it happened and was just not mentioned in the story; either way, shame was certainly brought upon that man because of his refusal to follow God's process. In fact, we don't even know his name. He was so concerned about preserving his lineage and making a name for himself, but in the end, Boaz is the man whose name we remember. He did the honorable thing. He followed the process. The elders of the land pronounced blessing on him because of his obedience to the Lord (we will talk more about those blessings in our final chapter). Boaz would most certainly want to tell us today that following the processes that God prescribes comes with blessings.

During my dad's stay in the burn intensive care unit, God taught our family countless profound lessons, many of which I have shared with you. However, when we look back at those times, we have quite a few funny memories we like to talk about as well. When you're in an intensive care unit for days on end with no end in sight, keeping up a sense of humor becomes quite important in the healing process. My dad definitely put his sense of humor to good use as soon as he was alert and mentally capable of understanding what was going on. However, in the early days when he was no longer on the ventilator and could speak again, he gave my mom and myself plenty to laugh about. He was still in a lot of pain, and was on several pain medications to manage that pain. Combining this with the fact that he was frequently going under anesthesia for multiple surgeries and the general confused state that comes with all the lights and beeping in the intensive care unit, my dad's mental state was quite humorous. Yes, we were concerned at times, but the doctors assured us that it was all a normal reaction to pain and medications; his mind would return to normal in time. So, in his oftentimes confusing ramblings, we humored him, and we chose to find humor in them.

Very early on, his ramblings centered on something he referred to as "the processes." Not a day went by that dad wasn't saying something about "the processes" and how we needed to follow "the processes." We had a hard time understanding what "the processes" were to which he was referring. My dad is a very orderly person; his life revolves around policies, procedures, and processes. Our first assumption was that he was either concerned about processes being followed at work in his absence or that he was concerned about the correct processes being followed in the hospital. However, within a few days, he was better able to articulate which "processes" we needed to follow.

He was quite concerned about the payroll of Butch Cassidy, Jesse James, Billy the Kid, and the other outlaws of the Wild West. Apparently he was the only one who would be able to follow the correct processes to make sure these outlaws were paid!

The doctors encouraged us to gently point dad to reality unless it seemed to upset him. One evening, when he was brought back to the room after having his last set of skin grafts, he started talking about the processes and the Wild West again. Dad had been suffering from a high fever for several days, so I tried to point him to reality by asking, "Dad, do you mean it's hot like the Wild West?"

I was quickly corrected. Dad responded, "No. We are *IN* the Wild West!"

So for that night, we just let him stay in the Wild West. It wasn't too many more days before dad rejoined us in Nashville, Tennessee, and now we all look back on that memory with laughter.

I realize that was more of a lighthearted, funny story, but it can be a good reminder for us all. My dad was overly fixated on following "the processes" for something as silly as ensuring that the outlaws of the Wild West were paid. This silly story really does speak to the fact that my dad is a man of order. Our God is a God of order, and He has certainly set forth commands for how things should be done. However, oftentimes we are not concerned at all with following "the processes."

We live in a world that tells us to just do what feels right, but this is always a recipe for disaster. God has created our world to be a world of order, and we will never get ahead by being deceitful or doing things in a way other than how God has designed. Thankfully, God didn't leave doing things the right way as a matter of guesswork; God has given us His Word, the Bible, as a guidebook for how He expects us to live our lives. Just like Boaz followed the process of becoming the kinsman redeemer that was laid out in God's Word, we can follow the processes God has laid out for us.

The most important process would be that of how to have a relationship with God. Our world tells us that there are many ways to God, and none of those ways are wrong. However, the Bible disagrees with this worldly philosophy. God is clear that there is only one way to have a relationship with Him.

John 14:6
Jesus saith unto him, I am the way, the truth, and the life: no man cometh unto the Father, but by me.

The Bible tells us that the only way to have a relationship with God is through faith in Jesus. Trying to take the easy way out, simply believing whatever makes us feel good, will only lead to failure.

Another obvious command of God that the world would tell us is unnecessary is gathering together regularly for church. The world today tells us that you can worship God wherever you please! If you feel closer to God in the mountains or at the lake, you can go there by yourself, and that can be "church." Although it is true that you can worship God everywhere, not everywhere is church.

> *Hebrews 10:24-25*
> *And let us consider one another to provoke unto love and to good works: not forsaking the assembling of ourselves together, as the manner of some is; but exhorting one another: and so much the more, as ye see the day approaching.*

I have had many meaningful moments of fellowship all alone with God, but church is designed to be an assembly. In fact, the Greek word, ἐκκλησία (ekklesia), from which we get our English word "church," literally means "assembly." If I'm all alone, there isn't much assembling going on; in fact, there isn't *any* assembling going on. When we don't follow God's plan of going to church, we miss out on the blessing of encouraging and being encouraged by other believers. The world may tell us it's not important, but God makes it clear that He has designed the assembling of the church as an important part of our growth.

There are countless other "processes" God has set out in His Word in order to help us live the most fulfilling Christian life possible. I could continue to list them, but I would encourage you to search God's Word for yourself and find what "processes" He has for you to follow.

What about the things that aren't specifically mentioned in God's Word? Those "gray areas" of life? God has made a special provision to guide us in the correct "processes" for those areas as well.

John 14:26
But the Comforter, which is the Holy Ghost, whom the Father will send in my name, he shall teach you all things, and bring all things to your remembrance, whatsoever I have said unto you.

When Jesus was gone from this earth, God sent a special gift to the believers: the Holy Spirit. If you know Jesus, then you are probably familiar with that still, small voice of the Holy Spirit. He is the One who helps us remember God's specific commands, and He also teaches us in the areas that may be considered "gray areas" as well.

It may seem like the life God has laid out for us is full of rules that we don't understand, but I don't want anyone to feel like the Christian life is simply about following rules; it really is all about a relationship with God. However, if God has clearly given us a "process" to follow in His Word, we can trust that it is for our good. In God's Word, He compares us to sheep time and time again. Sheep aren't very intelligent; they are dependent on their shepherd. It's time for us to realize that we really don't know what's best for ourselves; we need to depend on our Shepherd for leadership and guidance.

John 10:10-11
The thief cometh not, but for to steal, and to kill,
and to destroy: I am come that they might have
life, and that they might have it more abundantly.
I am the good shepherd: the good shepherd giveth
his life for the sheep.

The commands of God, the "processes" laid out in His Word, are for our protection. We simply need to believe that God knows more than we do. The reality is, I wouldn't want to follow a God that didn't know more than I do. The "rules" He has put in our lives are simply for our protection; they are a part of the path that leads to an abundant life.

I know Boaz would tell you that following the processes set forth in God's Word was worth it; I'm sure he thought it was worth it to not try to deceitfully get his own way. He followed "the processes," and God blessed him with an abundant life married to the woman he loved. In fact, there were more blessings in store for him than he could have ever imagined!

If you want to have an abundant life, follow the processes. Do things the right way. Do things God's way.

QUESTIONS FOR DISCUSSION

1. What are some of "the processes" laid out in God's Word that you know He wants you to follow? What can you do to better follow those specific commands?

2. Can you think of a time in your life when God blessed you for following the specific commands in His Word?

3. What are some things that may be considered "gray areas," but you can sense the Holy Spirit guiding you in the way God would have you to handle those areas?

Chapter 12

HAPPILY EVER AFTER
— AT LAST!

Happily Ever After
Is always worth the wait;
God gives love and laughter,
And He never is late.

Ruth 4:13-16
So Boaz took Ruth, and she was his wife: and when
he went in unto her, the LORD gave her concep-
tion, and she bare a son. And the women said unto
Naomi, Blessed be the LORD, which hath not left
thee this day without a kinsman, that his name
may be famous in Israel. And he shall be unto thee
a restorer of thy life, and a nourisher of thine old
age: for thy daughter in law, which loveth thee,
which is better to thee than seven sons, hath born
him. And Naomi took the child, and laid it in her

bosom, and became nurse unto it.

Finally! The wedding bells are ringing for Ruth and Boaz. Not only do they get to live happily ever after, but God also blesses them with a son very quickly. Giving birth to a son was the highest honor a woman could dream of in Ruth's day. This was not only a blessing to Ruth, but it was also a blessing to Naomi. They weren't calling her "bitter" now; the hope that was brought into her life by the arrival of a son to carry on the family name had restored pleasantness to her life once more. In all the changes their family had gone through, God had proven that He was the same, and He had a good plan all along.

Ruth's dreams were finally being realized, and she was getting to live her dreams with Boaz, her love. I'm sure that looking back on it, she saw the worth in her time of waiting. However, if she was anything like I am, I'm sure she wondered why things had taken so long, even in the days leading up to her wedding.

Sometimes things just take a little longer than we think they should; in Ruth's case, I'm sure she would have wanted to meet Boaz sooner. I'm sure she would have wanted to know from the beginning of her days of gleaning that he was the kinsman redeemer she was destined to marry. I'm sure she would have wanted their marriage and wonderful life together to begin earlier. However, God had other plans. His plan for her waiting was not because He was being cruel and wanted her to be lonely for as long as possible; it was just that He had some very important lessons to teach her in her time of waiting. He also had important lessons to teach us through her story thousands of years later. If God brought Ruth to the happily ever after without all the lessons in between, we would have all missed out on some amazing opportunities to grow. The way in which God orchestrated the story of Ruth's life was for our good and for His glory, even when Ruth didn't understand why things were taking so long. Ironically, in my life right now, the writing of a story has taken much longer than I originally thought it would. The story I'm referring to is the one you're reading right now: this book.

When I started writing, I had an idealistic picture of how all the words would fall right into place and I would finally be able to use my writing to be a blessing to others. After all, God had called me to write this story; it should just come together effortlessly. If only I could go back and tell newlywed Michelle just how wrong she was.

At the beginning, the words *did* come relatively easily. The stories God had put on my heart to share poured out effortlessly and quickly filled blank pages. However, after a few weeks, my writing began to slow down. Although it is true that I became much more busy with helping my husband in his ministry and this slowed down my writing, the biggest reason for my slowed progress was that the stories I was to share weren't coming to my heart as quickly. Sometimes I would go weeks without writing; sometimes it was months. There were many times I became discouraged. But looking back from where I am now, I'm glad it took me so long. At the beginning of the writing process, I thought the whole reason God had called me to write a book was so that I could share the lessons He had taught me with others. I thought that the finished product of a published book was the only important objective. I had no idea that the lessons God would teach me through the writing process would be just as important.

I suppose it was only natural that I thought once I got married and started serving the Lord with my husband everything would just be sunshine and rainbows. I mean, that was what God had called me to do! Wouldn't doing that be the ultimate fulfillment? Looking back, I can see how foolish I was to think that there was one simple final destination.

Don't misunderstand me, being married to Steven and getting to help him in the ministry is the most fulfilling experience I've had in my entire life. Moving cross country was a bit stressful because I had never really moved before, but once we were settled into our new home, I had an absolute confidence I was exactly where I belonged. I was doing exactly what I was supposed to be doing. But there was still something missing.

I remember so clearly that day in Greek class when God whispered in my ear, *"This is not what I made you to do."* In my brokenness, He showed me what He did make me to do. However, I didn't realize until recently that being a wife and mother wasn't *all* God made me to do. There really was something else; He just didn't tell me in that moment because I didn't really need to know yet.

After living in Utah a few months, I began to question my purpose again. It wasn't that I wasn't enjoying all the things God was allowing me to do; it was just that I had this deep sense in my heart that there was something *more*. God had a greater purpose for my life. Strangely, it took quite a while for me to discover the purpose He was trying to show me. I say "strangely" because the purpose He was trying to show me all along was a passion He allowed me to develop as a child.

The story I'm about to share isn't one I remember very well because I was young, and at the time it probably didn't seem significant to me. However, it's a story that my mom has shared many times over the years.

One day in the fourth grade, I came home from school and announced to my mom that I had signed up to be a part of a fine arts speech competition. For those reading that statement now, there probably isn't much of a shock factor that comes with it, but if you knew me as a child, you would understand why that statement came as a shock to my mom. I wasn't a quiet child; I was a silent child. I was just about as shy as humanly possible. Those who know me now may think I'm shy or quiet, but compared to myself as a child, I am extremely outgoing. God has brought me a long way in that respect. So when shy little Michelle came home and announced her interest in speech competition, the conversation went something like this:

"Michelle, do you know what speech competition is?"

"Yes, it's where you get up in front of people and tell a story."

I knew exactly what it was. And something in my nine year old heart burned with a desire to get up in front of people and tell a story. So that's exactly what I did. And I did it every single year until I graduated high school. Whether I realized it or not, I actually took every opportunity that came my way to tell stories. I started writing for our school newspaper in the eighth grade, and in the ninth grade I had the opportunity to become the editor. I always wrote at least three articles myself every issue; one article was a Christian fiction story published under a pen name. I love telling stories.

Even when I didn't realize it, telling stories was a theme in my life. When we moved to Utah, I quickly found a way to start telling stories; I had the privilege of sharing a missionary story with the kids in our children's church class for quite some time. It still amazes me how long it took me to realize just how important telling stories is in my life. I remember one night early in our marriage when I was really struggling with the feeling that there was something missing. I was believing Satan's lie that I wasn't really good at anything. Steven told me that night, "You're good at telling stories." That was *not* what I wanted to hear. Somehow telling stories just seemed very unimportant. Besides, there were only a few very limited ways I could use storytelling for God. I can now recognize that as another lie from Satan. When I opened myself up to use the gift God had given me, He started showing me so many different ways I could use storytelling for Him. I can't believe I didn't suspect earlier that God had created me with a passion for storytelling for a reason: to tell stories in as many ways as possible in order to bring Him glory.

At last, another very important purpose for my life became clear to me, and it rang out in one word: *storyteller.* I'm a storyteller. That word has become somewhat of a theme for this season of my life. I actually had the word *storyteller* engraved on a ring that I now wear as a reminder of one of the purposes for which God put me on this earth. I find such great fulfillment in telling stories that bring glory to God. Stories are so very powerful; do you remember the parables? Jesus was the master storyteller, and we still tell the stories He told because of how masterfully they illustrate the truth of God.

It's a bit ironic that God chose to slow down the process of the writing of this book in order to show me that He created me to be a storyteller, but I couldn't finish telling this story until He finished the story He was writing in my own life for me to share with you. My heart thrills knowing that the "happily ever after" of finally being used of God to write a book is just around the corner. It took a little longer than I thought it would, but the lessons God taught me in the midst of the process have been invaluable. In fact, I believe that many times in life the "happily ever after" doesn't just come at the end of the story; the "happily every after" can be found all along the journey. The part of my story that involves writing this book may be drawing to a close, but I know God has so much more to teach me in the next season of my life.

You may or may not have noticed the poem at the beginning of this book, but it's a poem that's very special to me. I wrote it in the eleventh grade just before one of my many speech competitions. I have often quoted it in my mind before giving speeches or being in plays, and I thought it would be a fitting beginning for this book. It's a simple statement that I hope will be true of every story God allows me to tell the rest of my life. I want to share it again here.

Today for God's glory
And not for my own,
I'm telling a story
With talents He has loaned.

QUESTIONS FOR DISCUSSION

1. Is there some end goal in your life right now that you feel like God is taking too long to fulfill? What is it?

2. What lessons could God possibly be teaching you during this season of waiting for your "happily ever after"? Do you believe those lessons could be a "happily ever after" in and of themselves?

3. Describe a time in your life when something took a little longer than you thought it should. Can you see now how God used that time as a season of growth?

Chapter 13

THE REST OF THE STORY
IS YET TO BE TOLD

I may not know now
How God will use my story,
But I have no doubt
It has all been for His glory.

The telling of the story of Ruth ends rather abruptly with the birth of her first son, but we are given a small hint as to the role the life of Ruth would play in the future of the nation of Israel. You might be surprised to realize that her life played an important role not only in the nation of Israel, but it also played an important role in your life and in mine.

> *Ruth 4:17-22*
> *And the women her neighbors gave it a name, say-*
> *ing, There is a son born to Naomi; and they called*
> *his name Obed: he is the father of Jesse, the father*

of David. Now these are the generations of Pharez: Pharez begat Hezron, and Hezron begat Ram, and Ram begat Amminadab, and Amminadab begat Nahshon, and Nahshon begat Salmon, and Salmon begat Boaz, and Boaz begat Obed, and Obed begat Jesse, and Jesse begat David.

Ruth's story was written long after her life had ended, but her name is remembered in history because of the importance of her descendants. It's easy to look over the genealogies when reading the Bible. I understand; lists of hard-to-pronounce names aren't my idea of enjoyable reading either. However, when God places names in His Word, it is for a reason. Behind every name is a story. The story of Ruth would hardly be complete without the list of names at the very end.

First, God directs the author of Ruth (who is traditionally believed to be the prophet Samuel) to go back to the ancestors of Boaz, all the way to Pharez. I find it interesting that God chose to go exactly that far back because Pharez has an interesting story as well. The latter portion of the book of Genesis focuses on the story of Joseph, starting in chapter 37 all the way to the end of the book. However, a little break is taken from this well-known story to tell the lesser known story of the birth of Pharez in chapter 38.

The beginning of the life of Pharez might be considered unfortunate, but we know that God always has a plan for every life. You may be familiar with the father of Pharez; his name was Judah. You probably know him as the son of Jacob and the brother of Joseph. Genesis 38 tells the story of a part of his life that was less than admirable.

The first mistake of Judah recorded in Scripture actually takes place in chapter 37 in the midst of a story that even children are familiar with. Jacob had twelve sons, but Joseph was by far his favorite. This doesn't seem to be much of a problem for Joseph's full brother, Benjamin, but it was the cause of extreme jealousy for his ten half brothers. One day when Joseph is sent to check on his older brothers while they were feeding the flocks, his jealous brothers formulate a plan to murder him. His brother Ruben can be given a little credit in that he did not want to murder him; in fact, he planned to return Joseph to their father safely. They threw him in a pit, and Ruben awaited the opportune moment to deliver him. However, it would seem that Ruben left the scene at just the wrong time; without Ruben there to protect Joseph, Judah proposed an awful plan.

> Genesis 37:26-27
> *And Judah said unto his brethren, What profit is it if we slay our brother, and conceal his blood? come, and let us sell him to the Ishmeelites, and let not our hand be upon him; for he is our brother and our flesh. And his brethren were content.*

Judah didn't want to kill Joseph; I mean, what would be the profit in that? They could at least make a little money for their troubles! So, with Judah as their leader, they did exactly that. They betrayed their innocent brother and sold him to slave traders for twenty pieces of silver. Then, to ensure their father would not find out, they agreed upon a convincing lie.

Genesis 37:31-33
And they took Joseph's coat, and killed a kid of the goats, and dipped the coat in the blood; and they sent the coat of many colours, and they brought it to their father; and said, This have we found: know now whether it be thy son's coat or no. And he knew it, and said, It is my son's coat; an evil beast hath devoured him; Joseph is without doubt rent in pieces.

Selling their brother into slavery was a terrible act in and of itself, but to make matters worse, the brothers decided to cover up their cruelty with a lie. Telling their father, Jacob, that his favorite son was dead absolutely broke his heart. The Bible doesn't specifically tell us how Judah, the ringleader of the whole ordeal, felt in the aftermath of this wrongdoing, but by his actions that followed, it is clear that this was the beginning of a very sad path for his life.

Genesis 38:1
And it came to pass at that time, that Judah went

> *down from his brethren, and turned in to a certain*
> *Adullamite, whose name was Hirah.*

Judah's response to the present turmoil that he had brought upon his family was to turn his back on them. He left his family to be with a friend. This was a friend who was not a follower of the one true God of his fathers; this friend was a pagan, and seemingly a bad influence. While Judah was dwelling with this friend, he continued to make poor choices that would affect the course of his life and the lives of many others.

In the verses that follow, we learn that Judah marries a pagan woman, a Canaanite whose name we do not know. He would have been raised with the expectation of marrying a woman of his own people, a woman who followed the God of his fathers. However, he chose to forsake his raising and choose his wife without taking into account what God would have him to do. He had three sons with this Canaanite woman; this is where his true trouble began.

When his firstborn was grown, Judah chose a wife for him, most likely also a Canaanite woman. Her name was Tamar. We are not told exactly what the wickedness of Judah's firstborn, Er, was, but the Bible tells us that he was so wicked that God killed him. As we know from the story of Ruth, it would be the responsibility of the nearest kinsman to then marry Tamar and raise up children for Er. This responsibility fell to Judah's second son, Onan. He did marry Tamar, but he selfishly did not want to raise up children in the name of his older brother. This displeased God, and God killed Onan as well.

This would seem to leave Tamar to now be the wife of Judah's third and final son, Shelah. However, as you can imagine, Judah was afraid of losing his third son as well. Because of this, he tried to get around the inevitability of his third son marrying Tamar. He asked Tamar to wait to marry Shelah until he was a little older, but Judah had no intention of ever following through with the promise of giving her his third son.

In time, Judah's wife died as well. He took comfort once more in his ungodly friend, Hirah. By this time, Tamar had realized that Judah had no intention of allowing her to marry Shelah, and she decided to take matters into her own hands.

She was told where Judah would be going that day, so she dressed herself in the manner in which a prostitute would dress in that time and placed herself directly in the path of her father-in-law. It probably says something about Judah's character that Tamar believed he would be tempted by a prostitute, but that is another story. The fact is, Tamar was correct. Judah did seek her services when he recognized she was a prostitute. However, her face was covered (as was the manner of prostitutes at the time), and he did not realize that she was his daughter-in-law. He offered to pay her with a kid from his flock, and she accepted. She requested three items that she claimed would be collateral to ensure his payment: his signet, his bracelets, and his staff. However, Tamar never intended to receive the payment. She only wanted his belongings because they would clearly identify him. When Judah sent the payment of the kid, she was nowhere to be found.

Three months passed, and Tamar is found to be pregnant by prostitution. She is brought before her father-in-law in order for him to decide what is to be done with her. His response? Burn her to death. Talk about hypocrisy!

At this point, the cunning Tamar produces the signet, bracelets, and staff belonging to Judah. He knows he has been outwitted, and he allows her to live. He regrets not giving her to his son Shelah as he should have done in the first place.

The time comes for Tamar to give birth, and it is discovered that she has been carrying twin boys. One of the boys put his hand out, and a scarlet thread was tied on his wrist. They named him Zarah. However, the other boy was born first. His name was Pharez. This is the Pharez mentioned in the genealogy at the conclusion of the book of Ruth.

Why would God put the name of this man with such a sad background at the beginning of this genealogy? I suppose I can't say for certain, but I truly believe God mentions Pharez in order to remind us that no life is too broken and no story is too dark to be used to bring glory to God in the end. Pharez is mentioned in another important genealogy as well. But let's not get ahead of ourselves.

In the genealogy concluding Ruth, we see a couple more names that you may be more familiar with. Let's take a look at the last two verses of Ruth one final time.

Ruth 4:21-22
And Salmon begat Boaz, and Boaz begat Obed, and Obed begat Jesse, and Jesse begat David.

You may or may not remember Jesse, but I'm quite certain you will remember David, the boy who defeated Goliath, the shepherd who wrote the Psalms, the second king of Israel. Ruth was David's great-grandmother. David appears in several other genealogies in the Bible because of his significance in God's overarching plan. Perhaps the most famous genealogy in which he appears is the one at the beginning of the book of Matthew. Ruth appears in this genealogy as well, as does Pharez. Perhaps by now you're realizing which genealogy I'm talking about. This is the genealogy of Jesus, the Messiah who would come to save them from all their sins. Let's look at a few verses from this genealogy.

Matthew 1:3
And Judas begat Phares and Zara of Thamar; and
Phares begat Esrom; and Esrom begat Aram;

Matthew 1:5-6
And Salmon begat Booz of Rachab; and Booz
Begat Obed of Ruth; and Obed begat Jesse; and
Jesse begat David the king; and David the king be-
gat Solomon of her that had been the wife of Urias.

We see several familiar names in these verses, as well as several interesting names that are new to our story. The spelling of the names is a little different in the New Testament because the Old Testament was written in Hebrew, but the New Testament was written in Greek. Nevertheless, it is quite obvious who is being talked about.

First, we see Judah, Tamar, and Pharez mentioned. What a messed up family history! But there they all are, mentioned along with Abraham, Isaac and Jacob in the line of Christ. We also see Boaz mentioned, but we learn something interesting about the mother of Boaz in this passage. Her name was Rahab. Her name is usually mentioned with a descriptive last name that you may be more familiar with: Rahab "the harlot." She was a woman with such an ill reputation that "harlot" is more often than not tacked onto her name as a part of it

Next, we see Ruth mentioned: the foreign woman

who suffered hardship after hardship, but chose to follow the one true God anyway. Her life was a broken one, but God allowed her to be in the line of King David, and, more importantly, in the line of King Jesus.

There is one more person mentioned in this portion of the genealogy of Christ who is quite interesting, and that is the the woman with whom David had Solomon. *"Her that had been the wife of Urias."* Uriah's wife. You might know her better as Bathsheba, the woman with whom David had an adulterous relationship. She amazingly appears in the line of Christ as well.

I've mentioned four women who were listed in the lineage of Jesus: Tamar, Rahab, Ruth, and Bathsheba. The interesting thing is, these are the only women mentioned in the genealogy of Jesus. They seem like quite an unlikely group of women to be mentioned! Why didn't God mention Sarah, the wife of Abraham who followed him to an unknown land? Why didn't he mention Rebekah, the wife of Isaac, or even Leah, the wife of Jacob? Surely these women were more worthy to be mentioned in the line of Christ! I can't help but believe that God mentioned the women He did for a reason, and I believe that reason will resonate with you as much as it has resonated with me.

The reason is simply this: grace. God wanted to show His grace in the lives of these women, no matter who they were, no matter where they had come from, no matter what they had done. He inserts their names into this genealogy to whisper in our ears that His grace is the same for us as well. It doesn't matter who you are. It doesn't matter where you have come from. It doesn't matter what you have done. God can still use your life.

The thing is, however, these women didn't know how God would eventually use them through the course of history to bring about the Messiah. Ruth, in the middle of her messy life had no idea how God would use her. Perhaps her purpose became more clear after marrying Boaz and becoming the mother of Obed. Perhaps she found great fulfillment in her life at that point. But there was no way she could have known, even at the very end of her life, just what God would use her life to bring about. The rest of her story was yet to be told.

Dear reader, I'm here today to tell you this: the rest of your story is yet to be told. Yes, God is still writing the story of your lifetime, but even when your life is over, only God knows how your story will impact eternity. I don't know about you, but that gives me so much hope, both for today and for the future.

My story hasn't been perfect. In many places it's been very messy. Sometimes it seems that even when I'm right where God wants me to be, doing exactly what God wants me to be doing, my story still becomes messy. One of those "messy" moments happened for me just a few months ago. I don't like telling stories for which I don't know a sensible ending, but I want to tell you this story simply because it *doesn't* have a sensible ending. It's one of those stories where "the rest is yet to be told."

I've mentioned before that God called me to be a wife and a mother, and I've shared with you how God provided a husband for me. During the writing of this book, God blessed us with our first child. Our baby was a surprise to us, but we know God knew about her before she was even in my womb.

Psalm 139:15-16
My substance was not hid from thee, when I was made in the lowest parts of the earth. Thine eyes did see my substance, yet being unperfect; and in thy book all my members were written, which in continuance were fashioned, when as yet there was none of them.

The news of our baby brought us incredible joy! The miracle of hearing her heartbeat and seeing her move on the ultrasound is a moment that Steven and I will never forget. The doctor said everything looked great; as far as we knew, everything was going according to plan, and we would be welcoming a little baby, our little baby, into the world in just a few short months. However, just three weeks after we heard our baby's little heartbeat, our story started to get a little messy.

I started having some concerns with my pregnancy, so we went to see the doctor to make sure everything was okay. Although the doctor said we made the right decision to come have the baby checked, she was very reassuring and told us that everything would most likely be okay. I think the doctor was the one who was least expecting what we were about to see on the ultrasound. Our tiny baby showed up on the screen, but she was measuring much smaller than she should have been. Where there had been a strong heartbeat just three weeks earlier, there was only quiet and stillness. Our baby had gone to heaven.

When God called me to be a mother, that's not really what I imagined my introduction to motherhood would look like. I never even thought it could be a possibility that my first baby would go to heaven before I could even hold her in my arms. In that moment I felt completely numb. I was just in shock.

We all know the truth: God has a purpose for everything.

Romans 8:28
And we know that all things work together for good to them that love God, to them who are the called according to his purpose.

I think that as believers, when something goes

"wrong," we start to look for the purpose behind it. We want to know why. We want something good to come from our pain. Remember the story of Judah leading his brothers to sell Joseph into slavery? Even something good came out of that wrongdoing. During his time in Egypt, God allowed Joseph to help prepare for a famine that was to come. Perhaps if Joseph hadn't been sold into slavery there would have been no preparation for the famine. Many people, including Joseph's family, would have died. When Joseph was finally reunited with his brothers, he told them that he saw the purpose of his hardship.

Genesis 50:20
But as for you, ye thought evil against me; but God meant it unto good, to bring to pass, as it is this day, to save much people alive.

Even in my moments of complete numbness, I started looking for the purpose. I didn't want a moment of our baby's life to be wasted. The doctor I saw that day was not my normal doctor. I knew that God had given me an opportunity to tell someone about Jesus that I would not have had otherwise. So, laying there with my heart broken in two, that's what I did. Maybe that's part of the purpose. But I doubt that's all there is to it.

In the weeks following our miscarriage, the numbness gave way to many different emotions; grief was definitely one of them. But thankfulness is another feeling that has been ever present. Going through Thanksgiving just a month after losing our baby, my husband and I agreed that she was what we were most thankful for that year. You may have noticed that I keep referring to our baby as "she"; even though we don't know our baby's gender for sure, we always felt like it was a girl. We chose to name her Gwenivere Faith. Gwenivere was a name my husband had always wanted to give to one of our future daughters. It was so special to me that he chose to give that name to our baby in heaven. I chose Faith because that's what our little girl gave me: greater faith in the One who is in control of all of our lives.

I don't like telling that story. Not because it's painful (although it is), but because there's not a satisfying ending to it yet. I want to be able to tell you that God used Gwenivere's story in a powerful way, and that I know the purpose of our difficult time, and that everything is alright. But I can't tell you that. Because the rest of that story is yet to be told.

A few weeks after our Gwenivere went to heaven, God blessed us with another baby. Although we had some difficulties at the beginning of the pregnancy that made bedrest and a season of "sitting still" necessary for me for several weeks, God has allowed this baby to stay on earth with us. Her name is Angela Joy, and Lord willing, by the time you have this book in your hands I will be holding her in my arms. I know God has a very special plan for the story of my Angela's life as well, and I look forward to seeing how it begins to unfold. But the rest of her story is yet to be told.

The rest of the story of my life is yet to be told as well. I have no idea how God will use my life, messes and all, to impact eternity. I have no idea how He will use the lives of the children that He will give me. But I know He will use me. He will use them. He will use all of it. And He will use you.

Dear reader, the rest of *your* story is yet to be told. Don't give up hope. Have faith. God has an amazing plan for your life. He wants to use your story for His eternal purpose. Stay yielded to Him. You may not see what great things He will use you for during your lifetime. I may not see what great things He will use me for during my lifetime. Ruth didn't see in her lifetime that God would use her to bring about the Messiah. But there is so much more to life than the short time we live on this earth. Eternity will be here before we know it, and then we will be able to see the amazing ways in which God used the story of our lives.

1 Corinthians 2:9
But as it is written, Eye hath not seen, nor ear heard, neither have entered into the heart of man, the things which God hath prepared for them that love him.

There is a poem that has been an immense blessing to me over the last few years as I have waited for God to do His work, and as He has been faithful time and time again to lead me. My grandmother slipped a copy of this poem into a letter she sent to me at college, and it arrived in the midst of a time when I wasn't quite sure what God was doing. I was waiting for God to bring the right man into my life, and it seemed like nothing was making sense. The words of this poem reminded me that God *never* makes a mistake, even when I can't see what He is doing. He is always the same, no matter how my life changes. I taped this little poem in the front cover of my Bible, and I have read it many, many times over the last several years. It is now taped in the front cover of my new Bible that has my married name printed on the front. It continues to be a reminder to me that God has never made a mistake in my life yet, and I can trust that He never will. I trust it will be an encouragement to you as well in your seasons of waiting. God is still writing your story, and He has *never* made a mistake!

He Maketh No Mistake
By A.M. Overton

My Father's way may twist and turn,
My heart may throb and ache,
But in my soul I'm glad I know,
He maketh no mistake.

My cherished plans may go astray,
My hopes may fade away,
But still I'll trust my Lord to lead
For He doth know the way.

Tho' night be dark and it may seem
That day will never break;
I'll pin my faith, my all in Him,
He maketh no mistake.

There's so much now I cannot see,
My eyesight's far too dim,
But come what may, I'll simply trust
And leave it all to Him.

For by and by the mist will lift
And plain it all He'll make,
Through all the way, tho' dark to me,
He made not one mistake.

QUESTIONS FOR DISCUSSION

1. Is there a part of your story that doesn't yet have a sensible ending? Do you have the faith to believe that God has a plan for that part of your story, even if you never understand His purpose this side of eternity?

2. How has the story of Ruth made an impact on your life, thousands of years after her death?

Conclusion

MISSING SOCKS AND GOD'S WILL

I have a very distinct memory of one night of my junior year of college. I was frantically folding my laundry in the dark at 10:45 p.m. in a manner that can only be replicated by a college student trying to make the most of the fifteen minutes left before lights out. I was down to just a few socks left, and as I reached the bottom of the laundry basket, I realized there was a problem: I had one sock left over with no match.

If you know me, you know I love having things just so, in an organized manner. You can imagine that a sock without a match was a huge frustration to me. It was even more of a frustration at college because with dorm laundry rooms, if you left something in the washer or dryer, it was pretty much as good as gone. It would eventually end up in the trash or the free box. If you got lucky, you could possibly rescue your lost item from the free box. But one teeny tiny sock? I often wear a child's size medium in socks. It could be mistaken for a dust bunny!

So there I was, sitting in the middle of my dorm room floor staring at the lonely sock in the bottom of the laundry basket. And as silly as it sounds, I found myself worrying about a missing sock! So I did the only thing I knew to do: I quickly got out my Hakuna Matata list and wrote, "Missing socks."

If you don't have a Hakuna Matata list, I highly suggest you make one. What's a Hakuna Matata List, you say? I'm glad you asked. You may remember from *The Lion King* the meaning of hakuna matata: it means, "no worries." (Hopefully you now have the song stuck in your head.) During my junior year of college, I decided to make a list of things I worried about. The goal was, however, that when I put something on that list, I left it there, never to worry about it again. A missing sock was certainly something I didn't need to spend any time thinking about.

Soon after this incident I found that I had another item I needed to put on my Hakuna Matata List. I phrased it this way: "What I'm doing with my life." It had become a question I asked myself frequently: "What am I doing with my life?" What I meant by that was, what will my life path be after graduating from college? Essentially, what is God's will for my life? I came to a point where I realized, worrying about God's will was not a beneficial use of my time. As I wrote this new item directly under "missing socks," I realized that "missing socks" and "God's will" actually had more in common than I ever imagined.

Worrying would never help me find my missing sock. I could have lain awake all night that night and worried until the break of dawn. But that would not have made my sock reappear. I had to realize this: it was completely possible that my sock was gone for good. Even if it was gone for good, I would eventually lose another sock or have to throw away a sock with a hole in it, and my socks would all have a match once more. It was also possible my sock would miraculously show up in the free box one day. Yet another possibility was that one day I would pick a shirt out of my closet and my sock would fall out from a clever hiding place it had chosen. The bottom line was, no amount of worry would change anything. I would just have to let the mystery of the missing sock sort itself out.

As I wrote "what I'm doing with my life" on my Hakuna Matata List, I realized that God's will shared many similarities to the dilemma of my missing sock. I could lie awake worrying every night, fretting over what God's will for my life would be. But that would not have gotten me to God's will any faster. I had to realize that God would reveal His will to me in His perfect timing. He was laying my path out one step at a time. And no matter how that path may twist or turn, He will always be the same, and He will be with me every step of the way.

Psalm 37:23
The steps of a good man are ordered by the Lord:
and he delighteth in his way.

God doesn't reveal everything to us at once; He only reveals the next step to us when He knows we need it. His timing may not have been mine, but His timing was absolutely perfect. *"He doeth all things well!"*

* * *

I did the laundry today. I now have a husband whose socks are mixed in with my own. (His socks are a bit larger than a child's size medium. They would never be mistaken for a dust bunny.) I got down to the end of my folding and began sorting the socks. I first divided them into his and hers, then I began pairing them up. When I folded the last pair, there were no spares. Somewhere along the line between my junior year of college and now, the missing sock issue sorted itself out. I don't remember exactly when or in what way; perhaps the missing sock reappeared, another sock went missing, or one sock got a hole in it, causing me to throw it away. I have no idea, because I stopped worrying about it. I stopped worrying about what God's will for my life was as well. And somewhere along the way, while I was busy in the barley fields and wheat fields of my life, God started to reveal His plan, little by little. Somewhere along the way, I became a wife in the ministry. Soon, there will be little baby socks for me to fold as well. There are still answers I could be waiting for, still things I could be preoccupied with and worried about. But worrying won't change anything. The end of wheat harvest will come soon enough.

ACKNOWLEDGEMENTS

I've learned that it takes a village to create a book. I would like to take some time to properly thank the people whose sacrificial help and professional expertise made this book possible.

To the Ladies of Faith Baptist Church in Layton, thank you for being my motivation to continue when I felt like quitting. I pray that this book will be a blessing to many of you.

Thanks to my sweet friends, Angela, Ashley, and Bethany, who were among the earliest readers of this book. Your heartfelt encouragement and constructive criticism made this book better than I could have imagined.

Extra thanks to Bethany for taking my picture for the back of the book! You are so incredibly talented!

Thanks to the community at hope*writers for giving me the motivation and support I needed to finish this project. You have taught me that writing is not a solitary act, but one that is best done with the support of others.

Thanks to Taryn at Typewriter Creative Co. for making this book a work of art on the inside and outside.

Thanks to my parents and my brother, Michael, for always being my editors and critiquing my work in an absolutely perfectionistic manner. Because of you, I'm always confident that my writing is intelligible and accurate.

Steve, there are no words to thank you adequately. You believed in me when I didn't believe in myself, and you came up with my title when I was too nervous to commit to one. This book would not exist without you.

My ultimate gratitude belongs to the God who crafted the story of Ruth's life and is still crafting the story of my own life. I pray that He would allow me to continue to tell stories that would bring Him glory for the rest of my days.

ABOUT THE AUTHOR

Michelle Elaine Burton is a youth pastor's wife and the mom of a beautiful one-year-old daughter. She has a Bachelor's Degree in Bible from West Coast Baptist College. Michelle lives with her family and their hamsters in Chattanooga, TN. You can find more of her writing at michelleelaineburton.com. Connect with Michelle on Instagram at @MichelleElaineBurton and on Facebook at https://www.facebook.com/ michelleelaineburton.

For a short reflection on one of the attributes of our unchanging God for each day of the week, download Michelle's free eBook, Yesterday, Today, Forever.

https://michelleelaineburton.com/
yesterday-today-forever/

Made in the USA
Las Vegas, NV
19 May 2021